100
FOR SUPP
SECONDARY EDITION

CONTINUUM ONE HUNDREDS SERIES

100 IDEAS
FOR SUPPLY
TEACHERS:
SECONDARY EDITION

Julia Murphy

continuum
LONDON • NEW YORK

Continuum International Publishing Group

The Tower Building   15 East 26th Street
11 York Road   New York, NY 10010
London
SE1 7NX

www.continuumbooks.com

British Library Cataloguing-in-Publication Data
A catalogue record for this book is available from the British
Library.

ISBN: 0–8264–8633–9 (paperback)

Library of Congress Cataloging-in-Publication Data
A catalog record for this book is available from the Library of
Congress

Designed and Typeset by Ben Cracknell Studios
Printed and bound in Great Britain by MPG Books Ltd,
Bodmin, Cornwall

CONTENTS

SECTION 5 Modern foreign languages

SECTION 6 Music, drama and art

SECTION 7 Information technology and business studies

SECTION 8 Humanities

SECTION 9 **Design and technology**

SECTION 10 **Physical education**

With love and thanks to C.B. – tea-maker extraordinaire!

Supply teaching in a secondary school comes with different expectations and challenges to working in a primary school. Primary specialists have been trained to teach the whole range of subjects and are expected to do exactly this if they are called in for a day or more to supply teach. They are generally given one class of children who stay in the same place, and they should have picked up at least a few names by the end of the day.

In secondary schools, however, teachers are often called in to cover lessons in subjects that aren't their speciality. Sometimes in secondary schools supply teachers cover one absent member of staff for the whole day, taking all their lessons and registration group. You may be lucky enough to be based in one room. Alternatively, secondary supply teachers may be given a number of different subjects to cover, filling in for five or six members of staff in one day, and moving around the whole school building. In this case, you could well have the same pupils in a teaching group more than once a day. The 'one worksheet fits all' solution you threw into your bag that morning won't be enough to fill the pupils' time.

As a secondary supply teacher, you may find that work has been set by the teacher and left on the desk along with the instructions, or that the head of department appears with a lesson plan or a pile of photocopies or books. Your job then is to keep the pupils on task and the pace of the lesson timed well enough to be productive.

However, things aren't always this easy. The head of department may be absent, based in a different building, or even unaware that a teacher is away. If the absence was unplanned the regular teacher might not have left work. Planned work might not reach you in time. And there you are, taking a class full of pupils you don't know, in a subject you barely remember from school yourself. The easy option might seem to be to 'baby-sit' the class for an hour, letting them draw or do homework while you make sure they don't misbehave too much. However, this means the day drags for you, and behaviour tends to get worse when the pupils are bored and unoccupied. By the end of the day you have a headache and no sense of achievement.

This is when you need a book just like this! Each section is designed for teachers who find themselves covering a lesson in a subject long forgotten. The emphasis is on providing activities to keep the pupils on task and occupied for the duration of the lesson, whilst requiring virtually no specialist subject knowledge from you. Some of the activities require minimal preparation, mostly the sort of thing you could squeeze into assembly time or at break, and you may need access to the Internet and a photocopier for some of the suggestions here, which is something that a school should provide for you.

The subjects covered in this book are:

o English
o Mathematics
o Science
o Modern foreign languages
o Music, drama and art
o Information technology and business studies
o Humanities: geography, history and religious studies
o Design and technology
o PE.

These are preceded by a general advice section, which covers the things you need to know when taking on supply teaching in a secondary school.

These suggestions should give you inspiration even if you have to cover a subject not mentioned here. Ideas for sociology or classical civilization could be gleaned from other humanities subjects, e.g. history, geography and RE. In Wales, you could use some of the ideas from the sections on modern foreign languages or English and adapt these for Welsh lessons.

Each section includes extension activities and work that will enable the pupils to carry on with the topic over more than one lesson. The ideas can be adapted for pupils of different year groups and abilities, and suggestions for how to do this are included where appropriate.

Once you have been supply teaching for a while, you'll start to pick up ideas and resources of your own as you cover the whole range of subjects. If a teacher leaves a worksheet for the pupils to work on, make sure to take a copy for yourself: you never know when you'll be called to cover that subject again. There are lesson plans galore on the Internet if you have the time to search, but carrying around a stack of handouts to cover every subject, year group and ability range, just in case that's what you're covering, isn't always feasible. This book is designed to provide you with enough ideas to start supply teaching successfully in a secondary school.

General advice

Many teachers who choose to do supply work cite the freedom and choice it brings as a major advantage. In secondary schools, short-term supply teachers are not usually expected to attend meetings or mark work. Working in a variety of schools gives you an excellent insight into how different schools can be, and you can pick up good survival strategies and behaviour management techniques. If supply work is abundant, you can choose whether or not to return to particular schools.

Some teachers take on supply work through necessity, sometimes until they can find a permanent post. Those seeking permanent posts may hear of vacancies when supply teaching at a school, and if you do your job well you will be noticed by those with the power to hire.

Of course there are disadvantages to supply teaching. If you do feel alone or uncertain, but have nobody in the school to turn to, make use of the online forums to be found on the Internet. The *TES* (*Times Educational Supplement*) has a forum attached to its website where supply teachers can swap ideas, queries and grumbles. It can be found at www.tes.co.uk/staffroom.

Supply agencies often have websites with an attached forum for their teachers to use.

HOW TO FIND SUPPLY WORK

There are a couple of ways to get supply work: through an agency or by direct contact with either the LEA or the school. Agencies generally cover a geographical area, and some have branches in many towns across the UK. You can register with more than one agency, and each will vary in the amount of work they offer you, loyalty schemes, opportunities for training and updating your skills, and whether they offer holiday pay after a certain time. They may have short and long term contracts. Agencies are paid by the school/LEA, take a proportion for themselves, and pay you a pre-determined amount. The amounts agencies pay may vary, even within the same area.

You can approach schools directly for work, and some LEAs have a pool of available supply staff, so it's worth getting in contact with the LEA too. Some schools like to build up regular supply staff who can get to know the school and its ways. It's cheaper for the school to employ staff directly than go through an agency.

For short-term supply work arranged with the school or LEA, you should be paid at a daily rate of 1/195 of your normal salary. This means that holiday pay is included in your daily rate. If you are given a contract for a longer period by the school or LEA you should ask how much holiday pay is included. If you work for half or part of the day, technically this should be worked out at an hourly rate, usually by dividing your expected salary by 1,265. The disadvantage of this is that you may not be paid for breaks.

IMPORTANT DOCUMENTS

Before you embark on supply work, make sure you have your academic qualifications to hand, as well as your teaching qualifications and your DfEE number. You will need to be registered with the General Teaching Council if you want to work in state schools, and this costs just over £30 per year. Sometimes LEAs might pay this fee for you: it's worth asking!

If you are working through an agency, they will advise you on applying for enhanced disclosure from the Criminal Records Bureau, or you can arrange this yourself. There is a charge, and clearance to teach can sometimes take months to come through, so make sure you are well prepared before you apply to teach. For more information on applying for disclosure, refer to the websites www.crb.gov.uk and www.disclosure.gov.uk, or phone 0870 909 0811. Once you have your disclosure certificate, there is no expiry date, but if you have a gap in your teaching service you may have to re-apply.

Another consideration is joining a union. Most teaching unions have reduced rates for supply teachers, and it's worth knowing that you have the back-up of their legal knowledge should anything go wrong. Look into what the unions can offer you in the way of insurance etc. If you do join a union, keep their telephone numbers to hand, as well as your membership number.

Decide whether you want to contribute to the Teachers Pension Scheme. Keep track of how much you pay in. Also keep track of your payslips or timesheets. If you work for more than 26 weeks of the year through the LEA this can count as continued service, and if you get a full-time job this will affect where you are on the pay scale. This applies even if you only cover a single lesson in one of those weeks. If you earn under the tax threshold in any tax year you may be entitled to a rebate.

If you have been into the school before you will know their procedures, but if it's a new school, you may not know more than the name and approximate location of the school when you receive your phone call. A local map and directory of school addresses is vital, and if possible get a contact name and telephone number of someone in the school you can call for directions or in case you are delayed. The school may be on more than one site, so if you haven't been there before, ring to confirm where it is you're expected to turn up.

Make sure you have everything you need with you – see the next section on 'Useful things to take with you'. Don't be tempted to overburden yourself, though, as you'll probably have to carry your stuff around with you all day. Leave plenty of time to get there: traffic is always worse around schools as the school run vehicles start to snarl up. You'll feel less flustered if you arrive at least half an hour early, but of course that's not always possible if you've received a last-minute phone call from a deputy head who has had a staff member call in sick.

When deciding what to wear, remember that some schools seem to believe that heating is for wimps, while others have hot and stuffy classrooms, so layers of clothing work best.

USEFUL THINGS TO TAKE WITH YOU

o Pens (black, red, blue), pencil, eraser, pencil sharpener, Tipp-Ex for personal use.

o Post-It notes.

o A notebook to write down photocopier codes, computer passwords, etc. Just don't leave it lying around!

o Biros to lend to those who haven't got their own. You can buy these very cheaply in 'pound shops' or in the 'value' ranges at supermarkets. Lend them out in return for something from the pupil to ensure you get them back. Or sell them at 10p a go, enough to cover your initial outlay.

o Chalk, board pens, board rubber.

o Tissues or wet wipes.

o A small bottle of water that you can refill at lunchtime.

o A flask of tea or coffee if you prefer hot drinks, or at least teabags and a mug. Not all schools have tea ladies brewing up ready for break time!

o Small change for schools that do have tea ladies. It's also useful for vending machines.

o Your lunch if you don't know the school (including the location and standard of the dining room!).

o Your timesheets. Copies of your qualifications, DfEE number and disclosure if it's your first time at the school, or your agency contract (just in case).

o A newspaper or book for lunchtime.

o Paper: A4 lined and plain – the school should provide this, but keep some on you in case you can't get any once you're there.

o Reward stickers or sweets if you are the generous type.

o If you know in advance what you will be covering, take along some worksheets to photocopy.

o A puzzle book to photocopy 'fillers' and/or a quiz book.

o Mobile phone with the school's phone number. Key in the reception number or the direct line to the member of staff responsible for discipline. With luck, you will never need to use it in a lesson, but it's there just in case.

o This book!

This book is intended to give you ideas when you start out with short-term supply work. You will soon start to learn about the topics generally studied by different year groups across the subjects, and will no doubt begin to collect your own assortment of worksheets as you are given work to use in lessons. You could begin to file single copies of these worksheets by subject and age group in a ring binder or concertina file, which you can keep in the boot of your car if you drive to work. Using ready-made worksheets from a school only really works in different schools though, because if you try to use the same worksheet in the school it originally came from, there's a chance the pupils have already done that work.

Resources that can be used in different lessons over and over again are useful to have with you. For example, in the section on modern foreign languages one of the ideas requires using pictures of people in a description exercise. Such pictures could also be put to use in other subjects like English. Start to collect a diversity of people pictures from papers, magazines and catalogues, and laminate them for durability.

Invest in a cheap quiz book, or start to compile your own quizzes that can be used with different age groups when you have ten minutes to fill. Other investments to look out for include a story book of myths and legends, a collection of comic poems, short stories that can be quickly photocopied, and collections of obscure/gruesome/bizarre facts about science, history and geography. All of these things should also be available on the Internet if you don't mind searching.

RESOURCES YOU CAN START TO COLLECT

Leave anything you don't need to carry around with you (your coat, for example) locked in the boot of your car. You will need to report to reception, and then be introduced to the staff member who organizes the cover. This is one of the busiest times of the school day, so do allow for that, and don't feel too unappreciated if you are left waiting around for someone to direct you! Feeling unappreciated often goes hand in hand with being a supply teacher, but don't take it personally. Regular staff members feel part of a team because of all those meetings they get to bond in; as a short-term supply you get to go home instead of going to meetings.

If you have driven there, check that you have parked in the right place and whether the school needs to write down details of your car. You may also need to sign in and receive an identification badge.

Your contact at the school, usually a member of the senior management team, will give you a list of the lessons you will be covering. You will need a plan of the school to find your way around, so check that you have the room numbers and that you can see them on your plan. Make sure you can locate the staff toilets, the staffroom and the place you should report to at the end of the day to get the day's work signed for and added to your timesheet. If you're working through an agency, they will have their own system for timesheets. If you have found work through the LEA or by contacting the school direct, they should already have a form to complete on your behalf and it will probably just need your signature. When you start out, ensure you know what you need to sign and submit to get paid! Procedures vary from school to school.

You should have been given your schedule for the day and hopefully a plan of the school, but also ask for a list of school rules or the discipline procedure, and write down the name and location of the member of the senior management team in charge of discipline. Make sure you know what to do with an unruly pupil: this may be filling in a discipline slip, sending for a senior member of staff or sending the pupil to a 'sin bin'.

You will need to know the times of lessons and when to expect bells and breaks. Also ask if you can have a temporary password for the school's computer system so you can access resources if necessary, and try to find out if any of your lessons are in rooms with computers, as this means you'll be able to incorporate the computers into your lesson. Try to find out if pupils have access to the Internet, or whether this is limited to a few websites.

Enquire about getting photocopies done: you might need a code to do your own photocopying, or be shown where you can take handouts to be copied for you. Some schools request that articles for photocopying be submitted to the reprographics office days in advance, but if you go along as early as you can and explain your situation the staff are usually very accommodating.

Find out where you can get lined and plain paper, and if possible keep a batch with you throughout the day. Finally, be aware of the school's procedures in case the fire alarm sounds. Each room should have instructions on display, and you should know where your exits are.

MEETING THE CLASS

Some schools have whole-school policies on how classes enter the room; in others it's an individual thing. Pupils may be expected to line up outside the room, or even in the playground. To make an effective impression, stand by the door to welcome pupils. This might not be possible if you are rushing from a classroom based on the other side of the school or if you get lost. Decide whether you want the pupils to sit in boy/girl formation. Some classes can be very unbalanced in numbers, so this isn't always possible. If you meet them as they line up, direct pupils where to sit in turn: the first to the left, the second to the right, and so on. This is a way of thinning out groups of friends and potential chatterers or troublemakers.

If the pupils are already in the room when you arrive, ask them to sit down and remove any clothing that isn't uniform. Tell them their bags should be on the floor, phones switched off and out of sight or they will be confiscated and given to the head of year, and the same goes for personal stereos/MP3 players. Also tell them to get out their pens and books. Invite them to deposit their chewing gum and sweets in the bin. If you cover all possible distractions straight away, hopefully the class will get the message that you mean business! Don't be unpleasant about this, though, otherwise you may as well have a target tattooed on your forehead. It's a fine balancing act! Be consistent with your instructions regarding what is unacceptable.

The class would like to know who you are, so write your name on the board. Also write up your starter activity and instruct them to make a start on it. This will give you time to organize yourself, especially if you have raced from the other side of the school, and to borrow two or three exercise books to see what the group has been doing.

You may have to register a tutor group (also known as a form group). Some schools have the traditional register, for which you will need a black and red pen. Look at how it's normally filled in before you start marking in circles or dashes or ticks. If you're not sure what to put for absent pupils who may just be late, leave it blank. Post-It notes are useful here: you can scribble a quick note to the administrator if you're not sure whether to put a mark or not.

Some schools have registers that are read by computers and must only be filled in by pencil, so make sure you have a pencil and eraser with you too. Ask the tutor group to sit down and explain you need them to be silent while you take the register as you don't know their names. Tell them how you expect them to answer their name so it's clearer for you, and if they don't look too uncooperative, you could ask them to raise their hand as they answer so that it's clearer still. Watch out for the whisperers you may not hear, the late-comers you may have overlooked, and the jokers who answer for other people's names.

Make sure you know where the register needs to be returned to, and ask a sensible looking class member to take it to the right place. You might have just five or ten minutes to register the group, or you may be stuck with them for half an hour. Perhaps use the time to have a quick team quiz: however much they protest at being told what to do if they are not used to it, most of them usually enjoy showing off their knowledge. Make sure you know if they normally have an assembly or something specific to do during registration time.

As a secondary supply teacher, you may find that work has been set by the teacher and left on the desk along with instructions. This is an ideal situation, though, and a sick teacher will be not able to prepare for their stand-in. If there is work, follow what has been set and, unless otherwise instructed, collect the work at the end of the lesson. If you tell the pupils that work is going to be collected, they will tend to approach it with more vigour than if they think nobody will see what they've been doing for the lesson.

If you can't find any work, send a pupil to the head of department or a neighbouring teacher to ask if they have some work for the group. Whilst waiting for a response, give the rest of the class a starter or warm-up activity to do: you will find suggestions for these in the subject sections. These are also useful to do while waiting for pupils to arrive in the right place, especially if you're in a different room to where they're expecting to be.

When the class is settled, tell them your expectations for the lesson so that they know what your rules are. Starter activities show you mean business, especially if you know that the immediate attitude of the pupils when they see a supply teacher is, 'Great! No work today!' Get them in the right frame of mind from the start. Having them work on something for five or ten minutes will also give you the chance to swap around potentially disruptive pupils. If the pupils walk in to find you desperately scrabbling around on the desk for non-existent lesson plans, or flicking through textbooks for inspiration, they will sense your weakness immediately!

You will need to register which pupils are present. You may have a class list with their names on it, or you may need to make your own list. You could send round a piece of paper for them to write down their own names, but you may get an abnormally high number of Donald Ducks in your lesson. To avoid this, ask them to get out their exercise books and have them on the desk beside them; you can then discreetly walk around and write down their names at some point during the lesson. Using this method means you can also make a quick seating plan so you can address pupils by name if need be.

Having a seating plan on your desk will also help if you have disruptive pupils. On the board, write the name of anyone misbehaving, and tell them this is their final warning before more formal action, whether this is being sent to a senior member of staff or being put in the detention book. You can also make a note for their regular teacher on who worked well and who didn't. Behaviour can be worse for supply teachers than for regular staff, but you can assert much more authority if you show you know what usually goes in the school, and name-drop the deputy head in charge of discipline, or their year head.

Schools can have very different procedures, but do use them to show the pupils you mean business and that they can't get away with substandard behaviour just because you're a new face. Make the most of your own tactics for dealing with bad behaviour: moving pupils, sending them outside for five minutes, and so on. Remember, though, that disciplining a pupil is often better done with a quiet word than hollering demands across the room!

DURING THE LESSON

Apart from organizing work for the class to complete (if none has been set), your biggest challenge of the lesson will be keeping the class working and behaving appropriately. Make your presence felt throughout the lesson. This is not the time for you to sit at the desk reading your paper! Circulate around the room and you will find pupils are more likely to stay on task and less likely to be tempted by mobile phones, sweets, etc. under the desk.

If a pupil doesn't appear to be doing much work, or shows you a page of work they claim to have already completed but which looks suspiciously like it's from a previous lesson, initial the margin of their book or paper and write the time to show where they are currently up to. Tell the pupil you will look again in ten minutes to ensure they are working properly.

Praise pupils who are working well. You could tell the pupils that you are leaving a report for their regular teacher or head of year with the names of those who worked well and those who wasted their time.

Move pupils to different seats if they are misbehaving or just chatting instead of working. Tell them they can move back if they work well for ten minutes. Once you have a seating plan with names on, write up the names of those misbehaving on the board. Let them know the consequence if their name is still there at the end of the lesson, but give them a chance to work their name off with improved behaviour or work output.

Make sure you know when the lesson should end, and leave sufficient time to pack away. If you have lent out pens, make sure you get them returned. Collect the work in if required. If the regular teacher has asked for the work to be collected in, don't leave it on the desk – this may not be their regular teaching room. Put it in their pigeon-hole in the staffroom instead. If it's work you have set, decide whether you want to show/burden their regular teacher with their work, or whether you should hang on to it if you are back in the school later the same week.

Tell each pupil they are responsible for the area around their desk, and that they won't be leaving if there is litter in their particular area. Watch out for pupils leaving rubbish on their chairs, or throwing paper into somebody else's area. Stand by the door ready for when the bell goes to stop a rush. Dismiss the tables or rows one by one according to how quietly they are standing.

If the class leaves a messy room behind them it's your responsibility to tidy it up. Minimise the mess by dismissing only those groups of pupils who have tidied up their area, whose desks are clear and who have tucked their chairs under their desks.

If a group of pupils has been disruptive, dismiss all the other pupils first. Tell these pupils politely and firmly what you expect of them next time you meet, and let them know if you are passing on their names to a senior staff member.

IDEA 15

CARRYING ON WITH THE TOPIC

When you are working on supply, you will often find yourself covering for a teacher who is off sick, so you could well meet the same classes if you are in the school for more than one day. You will therefore need an armoury of tricks up your sleeve: the same worksheet or topic is not going to pacify the same class twice!

In an ideal world, another teacher in that department would come rushing in with textbook references or prepared worksheets, but as this doesn't always happen, there are things you can do (covered in the subject sections below) to carry the topic over more than one lesson. If you're not sure how many times you might bump into a class over a week, you could start some project work with them; again, there are various suggestions for this in subject sections.

Another approach is to borrow some ideas often used by primary supply teachers. Teachers covering in a primary school often have the same class for the whole day and must cover literacy, numeracy, science, art, history, geography, etc. They will go in to the school with a project in mind, such as 'Patterns', 'Living things', 'Time' or 'An ideal world'. You could build up some schemes of work around themes and target each of them to the range of subjects; this may be something for you to do during any slack time you find yourself experiencing in a day's supply teaching.

There may be occasions when you need a ten-minute time-filler during a lesson: if the pupils finish the set work early, for example, or if you're waiting for the head of department to bring you work. Here are some ideas to use during any lesson.

○ Code making and breaking. Write the alphabet on the board. Invite a pupil to allocate a number to each letter. Each pupil should write a short message in the code. They can be swapped for partners to decipher, or choose one coded message to write on the board for the class to decode. To make this tougher, ask each pupil to make their own code and let them see if their partner can crack it by looking for commonly repeated combinations and letters.

○ Write up a (long) word on the board, e.g. 'experiment' in a science lesson or 'triangles' in mathematics. Challenge the pupils to make as many words as they can, using each letter only once.

○ Ask each pupil to make an acrostic poem using their own name, where each letter of their name is the start of a new line in their poem. This will help you to remember some of their names too.

○ Write up a number on the board and tell them this is the answer. Ask the pupils to come up with as many questions to that answer as they can. For example if the answer is 21, the questions could be 7×3, $1 + 20$, etc.

○ Chain letters. Write up some words on the board with a gap in between each. The pupils must find a word that starts with the last letter of the first word and finishes with the first letter of the second word, and so on. For example, if you write up 'station' and 'train', the pupils must find a word starting with 'n' and finishing with 't'. Make it tougher by sticking to a theme: in this case, insisting the word is transport related.

BE SEASONALLY AWARE

If you are supply teaching towards the end of term, be aware that the pupils will be starting to wind down. Some schools insist that regular teaching carries on until the end of term, whereas others have rehearsals for productions or off-curriculum activity days.

You can still provide structured lessons if you find this is better for behaviour management, but you can get into the spirit of things by using themed lessons, e.g. Christmas, summer, Valentine's Day, May Day. A good calendar or diary will inform you of the lesser known celebrations too. Just be careful if you are going into a specialist school, such as a religious school. Delivering themed lessons on the subject of food during Ramadan is not going to be much comfort to any children who are fasting, and pupils in a Jewish school will find more empathy with Hanukah-themed lessons rather than Christmas themes.

As exam time approaches, GCSE groups can always use revision and study techniques lessons, and newspapers around this time often have study guide pull-outs that you could photocopy and use in the first half of a lesson before giving them time to revise.

If you read a daily paper, look out for funny stories or controversial articles that you can use in lessons to make your teaching more topical. An article about an archaeological discovery could be a starting point in a history lesson or inspiration for creative writing in English or even MFL. Reports of a natural disaster can be investigated in science or geography lessons. Social issues could start debates in PSE, geography and sociology, and unusual business start-ups or success stories can be scrutinized in business studies.

There are lots of website recommendations throughout this book, which you can use to access resources and download worksheets. Some of them could be used in lessons, providing you have access to the technology. Very often you will only discover what is available for your use once you arrive in the classroom, so you should always have something paper-based for the pupils to do, even if you are timetabled in a computer suite.

Schools differ in the amount of access pupils have to computers. In some schools pupils are not allowed access to the Internet, whereas in others they might have access to only a handful of sites. Some schools allow pupils greater access to the Internet as they move up the school, and you may find in any one class that one pupil has been suspended from computer use for abusing the system. Be aware that pupils will try to use other people's passwords to gain greater access: let them know that you know what goes on!

Some rooms with computers only have enough to use them in rotation. Don't rely on printouts during the lesson: there may not be a printer, and if there is one it may not work or have enough ink or paper.

If you are planning on showing a video or DVD you will also need a back-up plan in case of equipment failure, double booking or non-existence!

BBC BITESIZE

www.bbc.co.uk/schools/gcsebitesize

This site has a decent set of revision notes and interactive exercises on 17 different subject areas for GCSE. If you find yourself with a GCSE group nearing their exams and you're in a room with computers, it's worth pointing the pupils in this direction.

BBC ONLINE

www.bbc.co.uk/schools/index.shtml

The BBC has invested a lot of time, effort and knowledge in their education website, and it's an invaluable resource for teachers and pupils. There are information pages, revision guides and interactive tests, worksheets and resources for teachers, games and a parents' section. This is a website you can use in the classroom, for example by showing animated diagrams or newsreels to the whole class on a whiteboard, or by letting the pupils take it in turns to access computers to work their way through the revision sections. Even the Key Stage 2 sections have items of use to secondary ages.

CHANNEL 4 LEARNING

www.channel4.com/learning/teachers/websites

A gateway to Channel 4's educational websites, organized by subject. Interactive games for pupils, resources for teachers, and lots of information.

TEACHERNET

www.teachernet.gov.uk

Search the database of over 2,000 lesson plans for Key Stages 1 to 3, soon to include Key Stage 4. These often have links to external sites, which have been categorized and reviewed.

In addition to the websites listed in the previous idea, the following collection will help you out if you are stuck for lesson ideas and resources.

TEACHER RESOURCE EXCHANGE
tre.ngfl.gov.uk/server.php
A huge, moderated database of resources, activities and links created by teachers and uploaded onto the site. Search or browse across subject and age ranges.

SCHOOL ZONE
www.schoolzone.co.uk
Thousands of reviews of web-based resources, searchable by age group and subject.

THE STANDARDS SITE
www.standards.dfes.gov.uk
This website, from the Department for Education and Skills, is where you will find general teaching articles and news, advice on special needs and gifted and talented pupils, and information on the Key Stage 3 national strategy.

CHALKFACE PROJECT
www.chalkface.com
A number of free, downloadable lesson plans and worksheets.

EDUCATION WORLD
www.education-world.com
A large American website full of activities and ideas for lower school pupils.

LESSON PLANS FOR TEACHERS
www.lessonplans4teachers.com
Another American site containing lesson plans sorted by subject, and many useful links.

TEACHING TIPS
www.teachingtips.co.uk
A publisher's website containing lots of free resources sorted by subject.

MORE RECOMMENDED WEBSITES

WORLD ATLAS

www.worldatlas.com

A world atlas of maps, flags and facts and figures.

KIDS R CRAFTY

www.kidsrcrafty.com

A site in English and French with themed activities for you to print off, such as mazes, puzzles and colouring pages.

CRAFTS FOR KIDS

www.dltk-kids.com

Printable craft projects, and you can create customised calendars in seven languages.

English

English lessons can be so diverse that pulling something out of your supply teaching box of tricks can be fairly straightforward. After all, we all speak English, don't we? So how hard can it be? The pupils could write a story, write a review, make up a diary entry ... all of these things come under the wide umbrella of English. However, setting one task at the beginning of the hour is unlikely to keep many classes quiet and on task for the entire lesson. Even if your task for the class is to write a story, break the task down into smaller chunks to ensure there is pace in the lesson. Give them ten minutes to create their characters, and then have some feedback. Then give them another ten minutes to sketch out the plot, then again have some feedback.

Try to find out from the teacher who tells you what you're covering for the day if the class is mixed ability or set according to ability. This should help you to decide what to do with the class. There are high-flying Year 7s who could finish a worksheet on apostrophes in ten minutes, while Year 10 and 11 lower sets would probably need the whole thing explained to them before they could tackle it.

Something to fall back on in English lessons is a handout on spelling, punctuation and grammar. Invest in a photocopiable book of worksheets, or print a batch off from a website. These handouts may not be inspirational, but they teach or reinforce valuable skills, and are usually self-explanatory so you don't have to be a punctuation expert yourself to use them. They can be simple enough to allow lower abilities the chance to work through them steadily, while higher ability pupils can use them as a springboard to more creative work using the lessons they have learnt in their own work.

Give the class something to do for five or ten minutes at the beginning of the lesson. This will give you enough time to establish what they have been doing with their regular teacher by asking one or two pupils or flicking through a few exercise books.

Write a word up on the board ('Constantinople' is a good one to use) and ask the pupils in pairs or small groups to come up with as many words as they can make from the letters of that word. They can use each letter only once, and you can stipulate a minimum amount of letters in each word. At the end of the time, ask them to count up their words, and then take in the list that claims to have the largest amount of words: if all the words are correct they can be declared the winners. If not, then take in the next longest list. This saves you checking them all!

A variation of this is 'Countdown'. You write an anagram of a nine-letter word on the board, and each pair has to make the longest word they can out of the available letters. Give them a time limit, just like the TV programme, to keep them focused.

You could ask the pupils to write a 50-word review of a TV programme or film they have seen recently. Choose some to read aloud, but don't give away the title. The rest of the class have to write down what they think the reviewer is describing. Have a trial run first, and once the pupils understand what they have to do, they can adapt their reviews to make them less obvious. This only works if they all watch TV, though!

If you like to be prepared, seek out some short stories to take into school with you. Get 15 or so copies made for your English cover lesson. It doesn't really matter what the story is, it's what you do with it that counts. The Internet can provide you with printable stories if you have none to hand, from myths and legends to short modernized Shakespeare tales, from the dark stories of Edgar Allen Poe to modern morality tales about topical themes such as bullying.

Having something to read together as a group sends a message to the class that you have work to do, and keeps the pace of the lesson going. Ask the group to 'read around the class', so that the first pupil reads a paragraph, then the pupil next to them carries on, and so on; you don't have to know their names to choose readers this way.

If the class seems boisterous then copying from the board is one way to calm it all down. After reading the story, or after each section, write on the board a number of questions based on the story. Pupils should write down the question and then answer it in a full sentence. You don't have to have prepared questions beforehand. Scan the story as you read together and jot down possible questions to ask them. These can be simple questions that locate information, such as 'What is the name of ...... on page...?' Lower ability sets respond better to questions they can answer, and once they are settled you can ask them more detailed questions. For very low ability, you could ask them to draw a picture of one of the characters, and label it with quotations or notes from the story.

Short stories can lead on to other work, useful for high ability pupils and classes you see more than once over a week. See the next section on 'Writing about texts'.

WRITING ABOUT TEXTS

You may discover that the class you are covering has a 'class reader' – a novel or play they are reading together. If they are a GCSE group, they might be halfway through reading an exam text or a book on which they will have to write a piece of coursework. Even if you have never heard of the book before, there are ways you can incorporate it into a cover lesson. This sends a message to the group that this lesson will be worthwhile, and that it's part of their regular scheme of work, rather than a one-off because the normal teacher is away.

In the first five or ten minutes, ask individuals or pairs to come up with a summary of the book so far. When they feed back their summaries to the class, this gives you a chance to understand what the book is about, and the names of the characters. Don't read on further with the class, because the regular teacher may have great plans for introducing a new chapter, character or theme, and if you don't know the story you are going to be lost anyway. Here are some activities you can do based on what the class has already read:

o Choose one character and make a character profile or fact file for them. Younger groups can include a picture or make a passport for the character. You can extend this task with the following idea. The story is being adapted into a film. Choose a famous actor to play the character and explain why they would be suitable. Design their costumes for the film.

o Write a 50- or 100-word summary of the plot so far. Compare the summary with one or two other pupils. Between the members of the group, come up with a definitive summary. Individually, sketch out what is going to happen next. Again, this can be compared with other pupils' ideas.

o Carry on the story from the last section read. Try to continue in the same style as the author.

Take a poem or two into school with you, or print one off the Internet to duplicate when you know you have an English class to cover. There are huge numbers of websites devoted to poetry by the famous and also by the less well-known. If you like your lessons to be topical, find a poem to fit the time of year: Christmas, the relevant season, Valentine's Day, holidays, Hallowe'en, Bonfire Night, etc.

Some poems are easily adapted to use with most year groups and abilities. Good examples are 'Jabberwocky' by Lewis Carroll and the ballad 'The Highwayman' by Alfred Noyes.

Once you have your poem, what can you do with it? Here are some ideas:

○ Before duplicating the poem, blank out some of the words, for example the rhyming words (if it rhymes!), or even every tenth word. Pupils have to work out what they think goes into the gap. For low abilities, number each gap and give them a choice of words on the board. You could either give them a choice of word for each gap, or write up the missing words in the wrong order. It's more beneficial for them to think of their own words, so provide choices as a last resort.

○ If the poem has verses (also called stanzas), younger pupils and lower abilities can illustrate each one. A variation, particularly for poems with old-fashioned or less straightforward language, is to ask pupils to provide a summary in modern English of what is happening in each verse. This task can be extended by asking pupils to divide a piece of A3 paper into boxes – the same number as there are verses. In each box, they can write their own summary of what is happening in that verse, and draw a picture to illustrate it.

○ After reading the poem, create some quick and easy questions for them to write into their books, along with the answers.

○ If the poem tells a story, like 'The Highwayman', pupils can rewrite the story in their own words.

○ 'Jabberwocky' is a poem full of made-up words. Ask pupils to create a dictionary to provide explanations or alternatives for the nonsense words. This is a great poem for them to illustrate, or to retell in their own words.

CREATIVE WRITING

For many pupils, one of the hardest things you can ask them to do is to write a story or poem. That's not because they can't write a story, it's because the instructions are too vague. They need ideas, and probably some help with structuring their work. Creative writing often comes after the pupils have studied some models of writing, such as a particular type of poetry.

It may be worth collecting together an example of an acrostic poem, a shape poem, one that uses alliteration, and so on. You can use these to show the pupils an example, and then ask them to produce their own. This is only really suitable for younger pupils, but most of them will enjoy creating their own poem once you have shown them how to do it, and if you ask for a poem poster on A4 paper, the colouring in and drawing can fill up the rest of the lesson.

If you're not sure what alliteration is, you may wish to avoid mentioning it, but it does lead to a fun activity of making an alliterative animal alphabet. Think of animals beginning with each letter of the alphabet: this task alone may take pairs of pupils a good ten to fifteen minutes. Then add an adjective to describe each animal, but the adjective must start with the same sound as the animal. 'Bouncing baboon' is acceptable, but 'gloomy giraffe' doesn't work, because the two words start with different sounds – the giraffe would have to be 'jolly'! Again, the outcome of this activity can be posters or booklets that can be illustrated.

Older pupils will feel more engaged if they write about something they're interested in. You will still need to be specific about what the piece of writing should contain, but pupils can tailor the subject matter to their own interests. They might write a review of the last film they saw, or (depending on their ability) design a new poster advertising the film. Ask them to write a letter recommending a place or attraction they enjoy, or a TV programme or CD. Give them a time limit to work to, though, or many will drift off task.

CREATING A GROUP STORY

If the class look like they can't be trusted to be left to their own initiatives, you can guide them through a teacher-led lesson with minimal resources. Ask them to get into groups of two or three, or randomly divide them into groups yourself. Tell the class that they're going to be writing a story in groups, and each member will take it in turns to write a section, while everyone contributes ideas. Each group will therefore need a pen and paper, and also either a dice or the numbers one to six written on scraps of paper and folded up so they can be picked out at random.

On the board write up six locations and number them one to six. For example, you may have 'the planet Mars', 'a desert', 'a city at the bottom of the sea', 'a medieval castle', etc. You could even ask groups to nominate the choices. Each group rolls the dice or picks a scrap of paper, and the number chosen gives them the location for their story.

Repeat this for characters: write up six different character types, such as teenage boy, an alien, a talking dog – however silly or sensible you want. Once each group has a setting and some characters, give them an opening for their first paragraph (for example, 'It was a normal day in (the place) and (the main character) was going about his business as usual'), and specify the time allowed to finish the paragraph.

You can use the dice and six choices to guide them through their story writing. The second paragraph could start, 'Suddenly a (something from the numbered selection) fell from the sky.' The story might end up being very silly, but this task will have given them some ideas about story writing and being inventive, as well as working in groups.

GROUP PROJECTS

If you see a group over several lessons, you could try the same approach to creating a group story, but this time as project work. Sort the pupils into groups and tell them that their group are, say, astronauts who have crash landed on an unidentified planet or that they were on a school cruise that has been shipwrecked on a deserted island.

Give them tasks to do, such as deciding how they will build or find shelter, for which they have to write reports or produce diagrams or maps. Throw in a wild boar or alien symbols and ask them to write a diary entry about discovering them. Each lesson or part of the lesson will have something new for the groups to encounter as they imagine they are the characters in their own story. For each new situation, they should produce some written work that can be put together as their Adventure Log. As mentioned above, the written outcomes can vary: diary entries; messages appealing for help; deciphering coded messages; diagrams and maps; inventories.

You can add an element of chance to their stories by letting the roll of the dice (or selection of a scrap of paper numbered one to six) decide what happens to them. For example, on day two they discover a cave. Write up six possibilities on the board, such as: a fire-breathing dragon emerges; they find a box full of edible food, and so on. When they roll the dice, they must include the event from the board that matches the number that comes up, and write it into their stories or diaries.

This type of project can last for as long as you want, until you decide that finally their group is rescued from the planet or island!

USEFUL ENGLISH WEBSITES

BIBLIOMANIA

www.bibliomania.com

Free online literature and study guides – there are short stories, poems, e-books, plays and articles.

TEACHIT ENGLISH RESOURCES

www.teachit.co.uk

A library of free teaching resources and news about English teaching, including competitions. Some of the website is only accessible through subscription.

LITERACY AROUND THE WORLD

www.warwick.ac.uk/staff/D.J.Wray

Ideas and resources for teaching literacy, including downloadable writing frames. These can be used across the subject range.

STORYTELLING IN EDUCATION

www.leraconteur.scriptmania.com

Lesson plans and downloadable resources on literacy and grammar.

ENGLISH RESOURCES

www.englishresources.co.uk

Hundreds of free teaching and revision resources.

SECONDARY ENGLISH RESOURCES

www.english-teaching.co.uk

This is a subscription site but there are a number of free resources.

ENGLISH AND LITERACY AT KEY STAGE 3

www.thegrid.org.uk/learning/English

Useful resources, starters and plenaries.

CONVERSE – THE LITERATURE SITE

aspirations.english.cam.ac.uk/converse/home.acds

Multimedia resources and games especially for GCSE and A-level students of literature.

ENGLISHBIZ GCSE REVISION

www.englishbiz.co.uk

Lots of advice on writing essays and understanding grammar at GCSE level, which you could print out and work through with a class.

SHAKESPEARE ON THE INTERNET

shakespeare.palomar.edu

A very comprehensive site full of background information and study guides.

NATIONAL ASSOCIATION FOR THE TEACHING OF ENGLISH

www.nate.org.uk

Keep up-to-date with issues in English teaching and new approaches to the subject.

Mathematics

Here's where I confess that mathematics is the area that sent me slightly wobbly as a pupil, and because of that lack of confidence it can still send me slightly wobbly now if I'm scheduled to cover a mathematics lesson. The advice in this section is really for supply teachers whose own knowledge of mathematics is but a distant memory, although even the more mathematically competent of supply teachers will notice that teaching methods and emphases seem to have changed dramatically since their own school days.

Luckily, many mathematics teachers seem to be on a mission to make their subject more popular and more accessible, and some have produced some fantastic websites for teachers and pupils to use. You can find out more about these in the section on Useful Websites. When you first arrive at the school try to find out if the rooms you are in for mathematics lessons have computers: if the pupils won't be able to access the Internet in their lessons you can sort out printing and duplicating worksheets in advance. Having a handful of mathematics worksheets, such as revision lessons on something they should have covered by the end of the previous year, is highly advisable in a subject like mathematics.

Peer marking mostly bypasses the need to demonstrate any teacher-led mathematics, but if there is a dispute and mathematics is not your strong point, there's no need to blow your cover straight away! Just invite the pupil to the front, and tell them to imagine that you know nothing about mathematics, and they should explain their theory in simple terms to persuade you that they're right.

If you want to brush up on your own mathematics skills, try some online tutorials aimed at Key Stage 3 pupils: lgfl.skoool.co.uk/keystage3.aspx?id=65.

Even if you have no preparation, you can start a mathematics lesson with some quick 'mental mathematics', a quiz in which no calculators are allowed. Fire off some times tables and get the pupils to write down the answers on strips of paper, which can then be swapped to be marked. Throw in a few simple questions of the type, 'what's the area of a square whose sides are 4cm?' These are usually aimed at primary school children, but they will allow you to gauge the class's ability in the first ten minutes.

Tougher starters include putting an answer on the board, such as 180 degrees, or 2x + 5, and asking the pupils to come up with ten questions that produce that answer.

You can find lots of useful starters on the website atschool.eduweb.co.uk/ufa10/starters. They have been designed for use with a whiteboard, but many of them lend themselves to being printed out or just copied onto a board. There is an invaluable booklet of 30 mathematics lesson starters to print at www.subtangent.com/maths/resources/30-maths-starters.pdf.

Some of the puzzles on this website are of the type 'Peter and Jane have 120 cards between them, but for every three cards that Jane has, Peter has only two. How many cards does each child have?' Once you start looking out for puzzles like this, you'll start to see them everywhere! Daily newspapers normally have a puzzles section that includes number puzzles, and the education press, such as the *TES*, has number puzzles every week, mainly for primary children, but they would still be a challenge to lower ability secondary classes. An archive of these brainteasers can be found at www.tes.co.uk/teacher/brainteasers. Start collecting number puzzles to use in mathematics lessons.

THE NATIONAL CURRICULUM

With a subject like mathematics, where the ability to solve problems demands a certain degree of knowledge, it helps the non-specialist to set work if they know what the pupils should have covered by their age. The National Curriculum website (www.nc.uk.net) states that at Key Stage 3 pupils should:

o take increasing responsibility for planning and executing their work;
o extend their calculating skills to fractions, percentages and decimals;
o begin to understand the importance of proportional reasoning;
o begin to use algebraic techniques and symbols with confidence;
o generate and solve simple equations;
o study linear functions and their corresponding graphs;
o begin to use deduction to manipulate algebraic expressions;
o progress from a simple understanding of the features of shape and space to using definitions and reasoning to understand geometrical objects;
o communicate mathematics in speech and a variety of written forms, explaining their reasoning to others;
o study handling data through practical activities;
o be introduced to a quantitative approach to probability.

Bear in mind, though, that a class's knowledge towards the end of any year should be more extensive than it is at the beginning. The point in Key Stage 3 at which these various strands of mathematics are taught does vary from school to school.

At Key Stage 4, a class may be following a foundation course, a higher course, or a mixture of the two. Some pupils will finish the work you provide very quickly, so be prepared to have something else to occupy them, like a puzzle. You could invite them to create a mathematics puzzle for the rest of the class to try at the end.

If you provide worksheets, pupils will work through them at their own pace, so you will always have a few who finish ahead of everyone else. Be prepared with some mathematics puzzles for them to work out, with or without calculators. Here is an example.

EXTENSION WORK

FOUR SAILORS AND A MONKEY

Four sailors and a monkey are on an island. They have collected a pile of coconuts, which they decide to divide equally in the morning, after a good night's sleep.

During the night Sid the sailor wakes up and separates the coconuts into 4 equal piles. There is one coconut left over, so he gives it to the monkey. Sid then takes one of the piles for himself, pushes the rest of the piles together and returns to sleep.

Then Simon the sailor wakes up and separates the remaining coconuts into 4 equal piles. He finds there is one coconut left over, and so he gives it to the monkey. He then takes one of the 4 piles for himself, pushes the rest of the piles together and returns to sleep.

Throughout the night the third and fourth sailors wake up in turn and do exactly the same as the first two sailors. The next morning the remaining coconuts are divided equally between the 4 sailors, with one coconut left over, which is given to the monkey (who now has 5 coconuts.)

What is the least number of coconuts there could have been in the beginning? (Hint: If there were 3 sailors instead of 4, the answer would be 79.)

The answer is 1021, and if the pupils plead hard enough, they can try doing this on a spreadsheet if they know how. Otherwise, it's a test of their use of algebra!

A simpler puzzle also involves monkeys:

THE THREE MONKEYS

Three monkeys ate a total of 25 nuts. They each ate a different odd number of nuts. How many nuts did each monkey eat? Find as many different ways to solve this puzzle as you can.

You can simplify this puzzle by changing the total number of nuts from 25 to 10 or 15, and make it more challenging by making the total 31 or 26.

If you want more puzzles, visit www.ex.ac.uk/cimt/ puzzles/puzzindx.htm. This is from the University of Exeter's Centre for Innovation in Mathematics Teaching and there's enough there to keep you going through a very long career of supply teaching!

'Countdown' is a numbers game from the Channel 4 TV show of the same name. You can play several rounds as an extended starter, or finish a lesson with this if the class speeds through the work set for them.

Ask the class for four numbers between one and 20 (or ten for lower abilities) and two numbers from a choice of 25, 50, 75 and 100. Write the six numbers on the board and get the pupils to copy them down. While they are doing this, perform your own calculation with the figures, using each number only once, and either adding, subtracting, dividing or multiplying them each in turn. You might find a well-concealed calculator will help you with this if you have to concentrate on behavioural issues at the same time!

Write your total up on the board, but don't tell the pupils how you calculated it. Their mission is to use the numbers on the board (no more than once for each number) and to get as close to your answer as they can in the time given. They can add the numbers to each other, subtract, divide or multiply. Ask the pupil whose answer is closest to (or the same as) yours to come and demonstrate their working out on the board.

The winning pupil can then set the next puzzle, which leaves you free to wander around the class and make sure every pupil is on task. You can add variety by insisting they use all the numbers on the board, or just five or four of them. You can have rounds that just involve addition or subtraction for lower abilities.

COUNTDOWN

SHOWING THE RELEVANCE

For this type of lesson it's best, though not essential, to have done some preparation. When you are confronted with a switched-off Key Stage 4 class in a lesson this may just be the thing to get them doing mathematics.

Collect together a set of mobile phone billing tariffs. These crop up in newspapers, in leaflets given away by phone shops, and are available on phone companies' websites. If you haven't done the preparation, it can still work by asking groups of pupils to come up with their own phone companies and set the tariffs they think are fair. Make sure you have at least four or five different tariffs.

Base your lesson on working out the best value for money for different users; for example, User One generally sends about four text messages a day and talks on the phone for half an hour at weekends; User Two sends about 20 text messages each week but talks on the phone for ten minutes during the day and an hour in the evenings, etc. Again, these phone users can be based on examples the class gives you. Encourage them to work out the average time they spend on the phone each week before they present you with any figures and you'll have managed to incorporate more number work into the lesson.

Ask the pupils to present their findings in different ways: graphs and pie charts, tables, etc. For something more glamorous, let them work on probability of winning at the casino: details for how this works for roulette are available at www.learner.org/exhibits/dailymath/placebets. html.

There are alternatives to doing mathematics when covering a mathematics lesson, and these don't require you trying to second guess what the class should know already. They are not strictly mathematics lessons, but on the other hand you won't be treading on the regular teacher's toes when it comes to setting exercises from textbooks or revising a concept the class has covered.

If you're happier with words than with figures, base your lesson on the history of mathematics. Prepare a simple comprehension on the history of the abacus (an informative website can be found at www.cut-the-knot.com/blue/Abacus.shtml) and then challenge the pupils to make or draw their own abacus. Discover the history of the Babylonians, who first divided days into 24 hours and each hour into 60 minutes. Their history and theories are available at turnbull.mcs.st-and.ac.uk/history/Indexes/Babylonians.html.

Find out about famous mathematicians at this website: turnbull.mcs.st-and.ac.uk/history/BiogIndex.html. Split the class into groups and have them prepare presentations on different mathematicians, for example mathematicians linked with art, such as Escher (www.mcescher.com). Incorporate art into the mathematics lesson by using symmetrical patterns to produce geometric pictures on graph paper. For much more information on the links between art and mathematics, including fractals, try the art gallery at www.math.ru.nl/knopen/art_gallery.html.

You could explore how the ancient Egyptians used mathematics to construct pyramids, and this website will tell you more: www.ancientegypt.co.uk/pyramids/story/main.html. Or you could show how they portrayed their numerical figures in hieroglyphs by using information from turnbull.mcs.st-and.ac.uk/history/HistTopics/Egyptian_numerals.html.

Most primary school children are introduced to Roman numerals, and will often only need a quick reminder of which letters correspond to which numbers. Give the pupils some simple sums to do using Roman numerals, or get them to work out the year that you write up on the board, just like they show at the end of television programmes.

MATHS LESSONS

www.mathslessons.co.uk/resources/resources.htm
This website provides links to worksheets from around
the world. It provides both a description of the contents
of the worksheet and also shows which national
curriculum levels it covers, which is extremely useful. A
high-ability Year 9 class would benefit from worksheets
aimed at levels 6, 7 and above, while low-ability Year 8s
would be working around the area of levels 3, 4 and 5.

MATHS ZONE

www.channel4.com/learning/microsites/M/mathszone
Here's a site for younger pupils to work through
independently if you have access to computers. It's an
adventure game testing the mathematical knowledge of
Key Stage 3 pupils.

THE QUEST OF NINE

www.learning-connections.co.uk/questof9/q_intro.html
Another adventure game for pupils to work through on
their own at a computer.

SUBTANGENT

www.subtangent.com
A website you can use to print out worksheets and
resources, or one to let the pupils loose on. It contains
pages on revision, testing yourself, games and
investigations.

MATH GOODIES

www.mathgoodies.com
An American site suitable for Key Stage 3. There is a
library of interactive mathematics lessons along with a
homework help forum. The teacher's section has
printable worksheets.

INTERACTIVE MATHEMATICS AND PUZZLES

www.cut-the-knot.org/front.shtml
Lots of mathematics puzzles that require distinct areas of
knowledge, such as geometry and probability. This site is
a useful way to show pupils practical applications of the
theories they are studying. Most of the puzzles are, as the
title says, interactive, so this is a website to use in lessons
rather than print from.

SUDOKU PUZZLES
www.sudoku.org.uk/backpuzzles.htm
These number square puzzles became a popular numeric alternative to crossword puzzles in British newspapers in the spring of 2005, and this site gives you a large archive of puzzles that you can print out, along with the rules. Logic is more important in solving these than mathematical competence, and by adding a competitive edge to the lesson these puzzles ensure the majority of pupils stay on task for a while. Either make sure you have spare copies for pupils who mess up their original, or insist they work in pencil.

PI FACTORY
www.pifactory.co.uk
Click on the 'Teacher stuff' link to find an incredible amount of resources that you can use in the classroom.

MATHS GURU
www.mathsguru.co.uk
Another website offering a vast amount of worksheets. You will need an Acrobat viewer, but these are freely downloadable.

Science

Of all the subjects taught in schools today, science is one of the fastest changing. You can't have failed to notice news reports about new scientific discoveries, progress in understanding genetics, and greater exploration of our own planet and the universe beyond. All this has to filter down to science lessons, so if the last time you studied science was a decade or more ago, you might be bewildered to discover some of the facts and theories that children are taught today.

For this reason, unless you are a science specialist or you subscribe to the *New Scientist*, my advice is to stick to simpler concepts that pupils should already have covered in lessons and base work on consolidating or revising that knowledge. The lesson ideas here require the scientific knowledge that most children have acquired by the time they reach secondary school, and you can use that knowledge to complete different activities.

With smaller groups and classes you know and trust you can have them compiling data if you don't mind them moving around the room. They can collect details about everybody, such as their age in years and days, or their height. Then they can use this to calculate mean, mode and median averages, and display the results as charts.

If you have lessons with older pupils or more able children you may wish to set them work they can complete independently, or you might want to read up on the subject yourself. If this is the case, take a look at the recommended websites.

Don't forget that science lessons will probably take place in a lab with lots of distractions and safety issues for you to consider. Have a selection of penalties at your disposal for pupils who mess around with equipment, and insist that pupils remain on their stools or chairs unless they have your permission to move. You need to have lesson ideas to engage them straight away, minimizing the opportunities for them to become distracted. The class may be expecting dazzling practicals or demonstrations, but don't be tempted unless you really know what you're doing!

CREATE A CREATURE

This activity is most suitable for younger year groups or special needs pupils. Start off by giving the class the names of different habitats, for example pond, sea, river, jungle, woodland and desert, or ask them to come up with a definitive list between them. Ask pairs or teams to come up with as many different creatures as they can think of that live in those habitats. Then comes the trickier part: for each creature, they must work out at least one way that it is adapted for its environment, such as thick fur on Arctic animals or gills on aquatic creatures.

Once you have completed the introductory work, the pupils now have their main task: creating their own creature by combining two animals from their list. You can make it more difficult by insisting the animals come from different habitats. Pupils have to decide which features of the two animals their new creature retains, and then decide on a habitat for it to live in. They can produce drawings or diagrams, with labels, of their creatures. They also need to explain how the animal has adapted to exist in its habitat: what it eats, how it avoids being eaten, how it finds its food, how it keeps warm or cool, whether it is nocturnal or aquatic or tree-dwelling, and so on. They could do this as a written report, or in pairs, or as a short speech to give to the rest of their group or to the class, depending on ability and behaviour.

If you still have time at the end of the lesson, you could use the work they've produced for more activities. One idea is to sort the pupils into small groups and tell them they must create a section of the zoo for their creatures. They must draw a plan showing which animals can live next to each other and which must be kept far apart, and also what kind of enclosures their creatures need.

Another idea is for one pupil to come to the front without revealing their new creature. The rest of the class must try to guess which two animals they have combined by asking questions that can be answered with yes or no, e.g. 'Is your animal a carnivore?', 'Does your animal like water?'

If you have computer access, visit the Classifying Critters website (www.hhmi.org/coolscience/critters/critters.html) for extension work; here pupils can try their hand at grouping animals and learn about classification.

Secondary school pupils should study the topic of planets quite early on, so most classes will have some knowledge of the solar system. As a revision exercise, ask pupils to look over their notes or the textbook pages and create a fact file about the solar system. You can add further requirements if you get the chance to look at their books and see what emphases their work took. Older pupils may well have forgotten what they learned, so you may need worksheets or photocopies for prompts. The form of their fact files will depend on the age and ability of the pupils: posters comparing planet sizes and colours, booklets with a page on each planet (they could work on these in groups of two or three), a sample textbook page including questions and activities for their peers or younger pupils, or essay style responses.

For a twist, pupils could make a 'Space Tourist's Guide', writing what it would be like for a visitor to the planet(s) of their choice. They would need to consider what protective clothing visitors would need and why, what they should expect of the planet's surface, how long it would take to get there from Earth, how long a day or year would last there, and any other information useful to a visitor that they can draw from their prior knowledge.

They could design menus for space travel by listing all the dehydrated foodstuffs that are available to us, and designing a daily menu for space tourists that covers as many nutritional needs as they can manage.

Follow-up work could include sending a postcard from the planet they've chosen, or creative writing in the form of a story about their imaginary visit. Other creative writing ideas include a diary, captain's log or scientific report of an imaginary visit to the chosen planet, illustrated with pictures of rock samples and so on.

If you want to print out and photocopy some basic facts and diagrams about the solar system, a good starting place is the website www.enchantedlearning. com/subjects/astronomy/planets. It includes a table of very useful comparative figures.

If you have access to computers or a whiteboard, you can show them NASA's Solar System Simulator at: space.jpl.nasa.gov.

For more lesson ideas to do with space, visit www.spacetoday.org/Teachers/LessonPlans.html.

You can use this lesson idea across the age groups because the outcomes will depend on the knowledge pupils have already accumulated. As a starter, ask the class to write a list of everything they have on them or that they can see in the classroom that's made of plastic. They can compare their lists in small groups. Tell the pupils that in each case plastic is replacing a natural material. Next to each item on their list, they should guess what natural material the item could be made from instead: wood, leather, cotton, etc. Once they've got the idea, tell them to choose a room in their house, and to list everything made of plastic that they can think of in that room, from light switches and TV sets to cables and curtain rails. Tell them to imagine that plastic is about to be outlawed, and they have to think of natural or alternative materials for everything instead.

Once they have their lists, items can be sorted into categories: objects made from wood, rope, cotton, metal, etc. They can guesstimate how much of each material they would need to replace the plastic items, and then represent this data in graphs or charts. They can then draw simple conclusions from this: what would be the environmental effects of needing more wood? What would we need to do to produce more cotton? More able and older pupils will be able to draw more complex conclusions about deforestation, etc.

They can write up their findings and conclusions into a report, with sections on items currently made of plastic, the materials that could be used as alternatives, any items that couldn't be made of non-plastic materials and would have to disappear, and the environmental, and perhaps societal, effects of using different materials. For the more creatively inclined they could use their data to write a 'what if?' story of a nightmare future scenario when plastic is outlawed because oil runs out.

INCREDIBLE JOURNEY

This idea can be adapted quite easily for different age groups and used for biology, chemistry or physics. The outcome will be a written piece of work, which can consist of a story, illustrated diagram, or something written in the style of a holiday brochure or tourist guide. Set the group a starter activity such as unravelling anagrams of key science vocabulary. While the pupils are warming up, take a look through their books to see what they have been studying recently.

If it's been biology they might have been studying the respiratory, digestive or circulatory systems. Ask pupils to imagine they are producing a travel guide for blood cells or food or oxygen molecules to let them know what they're in for during their journey round the body. The guide should consist of a description of what happens as well as selected pictures or diagrams. This idea can be adapted to other areas of study. In biology they might have been learning about the life cycle of a plant or creature, and this can also be written about in travelogue style.

In chemistry the pupils might have been studying the water, rock or nitrogen cycles, all topics that are easily adapted to producing a travel guide. The journey of ores or chemicals in the process of extracting aluminium or iron, for example, can also be reported in this form. Some topics may require a little more imagination. Pupils may have been learning about reactivity of metals or non-metals, or the properties of groups of elements from the periodic table. In this case, the journey they write about can be from the point of view of an atom or group of atoms: what happens when they encounter fire, water, other elements or acids. If you compile a list on the board of the experiments they have carried out and the theories they have studied, it can serve as a checklist for the whole class to ensure they have included enough details in their own piece of work. The detail in which pupils produce their guide will depend on their age group: younger pupils may just know that a chemical turns a particular colour when it encounters another chemical, while GCSE pupils should be able to draw diagrams of molecular and atomic structures.

Examples for physics may include describing the journey of an electrical current around a circuit or the transfer of energy between different forms: from potential to kinetic to thermal. Pupils could write about the journey of light to the eye and how images are processed by the brain. The important thing here is that you don't have to introduce anything new to the pupils, but you are helping them to consolidate knowledge they already have by writing about it in a different way.

SCHOOL SCIENCE

www.schoolscience.co.uk/content/index.asp

An extremely comprehensive site featuring animations and illustrations, pages of information and interactive quizzes, teachers' support and worksheets, and it's conveniently divided into Key Stages. You could use it to make yourself a ready-to-photocopy teaching pack for science lessons.

TEACHING TIPS

www.teachingtips.co.uk

o Follow the links to secondary science. There's a glossary of terms that you could use for word games as a starter activity.

o Print out the diagrams of the heart or digestive system (there are others too) and ask the pupils to copy and/or label them. If you have access to textbooks this could be an investigative activity. Answers are provided on the site, so you could just give them the words with which to label the diagram.

o There are data tables, e.g. of vitamins and minerals. Print these in advance and blank out some of the boxes for the pupils to fill in, or muddle up the headings so it becomes a mix and match exercise.

o There are comprehensive biographies at the 'Scientist of the Month' section, which you can print out and use to make fact files, posters or wall displays.

GREAT BARR SCHOOL

web.greatbarr.bham.sch.uk/science/powerpoint.htm

o There's a wealth of useful resources for teaching science in this school's website, in particular a selection of substantial PowerPoint presentations that can be downloaded. They cover biology, chemistry and physics from Key Stages 3 to 5, and would be a suitable starting place for a lesson if you have access to computers and/or a whiteboard. Alternatively, you could print out copies.

o There's an 'online laboratory' which consists of interactive diagrams and movies to demonstrate points across the three sciences.

- There's also a section on starters and plenaries with files allowing you to generate your own card games and use computer-based quizzes.
- Revision sheets are available for topics across Key Stages 3 and 4.

SCIENCE UPDATE
www.upd8.org.uk
A useful resource for older or more able pupils, this website features current hot topics in science and provides related worksheets if you register.

SCIENCE DEBATES
www.scienceyear.com/sciteach/index.html?page=/sciteach/debating/index.html
This link provides you with resources to run a debate in the classroom, with PDF files containing teacher notes, worksheets for the pupils and research handouts on the topic areas. Spend a lesson with groups of pupils preparing to debate for or against the introduction of pink Brussels sprouts to the school canteen, which covers the issue of genetically modified food. This Planet Science website also has a large number of other resources for you to browse, such as printable worksheets on whether you can really become a burger addict, and acid bath murderers (not for the faint hearted!).

INTERACTIVE PERIODIC TABLE

www.webelements.co.uk

Click on the elements to be taken to highly informative fact-filled pages. Use the website for an investigation during lessons or print out some of the details in advance to use in activities.

CHEMISTRY FOR KIDS

www.chem4kids.com

This is like an online textbook: useful if you need access to facts for Key Stage 4 pupils. Print the information out in advance or let them access it via computers. You could make up some simple questions to test whether they have understood what they've read, or ask them to make up their own questions to test other class members. They could make revision notes or represent the information in different ways, e.g. as diagrams.

CREATIVE CHEMISTRY

www.creative-chemistry.org.uk/funstuff/xword/index.htm

Ready-made crosswords for you to print out if you have time to prepare. You'll also find wordsearches that can be completed online or printed out, jigsaws and all sorts of quizzes and puzzles.

PLANET DIARY

www.phschool.com/science/planetdiary/index.html

You can use this in lessons if you have access to computers or a whiteboard. A clickable map of the world allows you to investigate news stories on topics such as droughts, earthquakes, volcanoes, health and astronomy. The activities link leads to printable worksheets to guide pupils through their investigations.

THE PHYSICS CLASSROOM

www.physicsclassroom.com

A site allowing pupils to work at their own pace through physics tutorials and then test themselves. There's also a visualization studio where pictures and animations illustrate physics concepts.

PHYSICS LIFE

www.physics.org/physics_life/physics_life_text.asp
This site explains how physics is all around us, from the
kitchen and bathroom to the playground and street. A
good starting place for investigations and project work.
Pupils could create information illustrations which could
be pieced together to make display work, for example of
physics at work in a living room or street.

HOW STUFF WORKS

www.howstuffworks.com
Sections include computers, health, science, people,
electronics and autos. If you have time to prepare a
printout for a one-off lesson, choose something you're
interested in: examples include fireworks, rainbows,
earthquakes, roller coasters, Bigfoot, cloning. Ask the
pupils to make up quizzes based on the information
they're given or present it in a different form such as a
storyboard or cartoon strip.

BIOLOGY IN MOTION

www.biologyinmotion.com
This is a site to use in the classroom. There are cartoon
mini lectures (the computers need to have Flash installed
for these), an evolution simulation, drag and drop
activities, and 3-D animations of biological processes.

Modern foreign languages

ANAGRAMS

Write a selection of the words from the glossary (see the end of this section) on the board, muddling up the letters as you write. Give the pupils a set time to decipher the words, either individually or in pairs. You could generate more vocabulary lists from the pupils in quick vocabulary quizzes. Going through the answers with the class will hopefully give you an agreement of correct spellings! Most pupils will have vocabulary lists in their exercise books, or in the textbooks. If you are teaching in an MFL classroom, there could well be displays of words and phrases around the room.

MEMORY GAME

This is a whole-class activity. Write the appropriate translation of 'I went to the shops and I bought ...' on the board (see the word glossaries at the end of this section). Ask the first pupil to read the phrase and suggest something they bought at the shops. The second pupil should repeat the phrase and the first object, and add their own object. It gets harder as you move around the class!

To make it trickier for older classes, limit the vocabulary they can use to a particular group of words, for example food and drink or clothes. You could also ask the first pupil to start with something beginning with the letter 'a', the next pupil with 'b', and so on.

To make it easier, each pupil could come to the board in turn and write up their chosen word. Encourage the rest of the class to use dictionaries or vocabulary lists to check that the spelling is correct.

MAKING QUIZZES

To follow the warm-up activities with some written work, the vocabulary generated could be used by each pupil to create their own wordsearch or crossword. It would be helpful to use graph paper. Wordsearches can be created by lower-year groups or lower-ability classes. Compiling crosswords is more of a challenge: depending on ability, the pupils could provide the clues in English or in the target language. You could then collect in their puzzles and photocopy them to use with other classes, or redistribute the puzzles to let them solve each others'.

MEMORY GAME VARIATION

This is similar to the warm-up activity, except it tests adjectives rather than nouns. Provide them with the phrase 'My friend's cat/dog/house is ...' (see the word glossaries at the end of this section). Once everyone has contributed a word to describe the object, ask them to draw the object using five of the descriptions, and label their picture with the vocabulary. Or, if they leave their picture word-free, they can play a guessing game in pairs with the pictures, with each partner trying to work out the five descriptive words chosen.

Having chosen five words, you could then play bingo with the vocabulary. Call out, or write on the board, a word at a time from the list generated by the class or, better still, enlist a pupil to call out the words. This is a better option if your language skills are rusty or non-existent.

'STOP THE BUS!'

This is another test of vocabulary. Give the pupils five category headings, which each team of three or four writes at the top of a sheet of paper. Categories could include colours, clothing, parts of the body, food and drink, animals, countries, girls' names and boys' names. When each team is ready, write a letter on the board. The first team to fill in a word under each category beginning with that letter should raise their hands and say 'Stop the bus!' You could appoint an official scorer and checker from the pupils. This game can last for several rounds.

For a quieter version that takes longer, use the following variation. Once you have written up the letter on the board, give the teams two minutes to think of as many words as they can in each category. Encourage them to be quiet by telling them that if they call out words to their team mates, everybody else in the class will hear. Again, if it's a language of which you have no knowledge, appoint official checkers from the class to add up the correct words.

VOCABULARY GAMES

CHARACTER DESCRIPTION

This activity can be used across the ability range. Language learners or low-ability pupils can use simple one-word descriptions, using a dictionary if need be. Older pupils and higher-ability groups can use whole sentences, write in the present or past, and create short stories about their characters.

This activity could follow on from a game that generates adjectives, especially if they have been written up on the board.

It's preferable to have some pictures to use with the pupils. If you come unprepared, you could still use this activity. You will have to ask each pupil to draw a character, making sure they give it a certain hair colour and type, eye colour and definite clothing (rather than stick-man blandness).

You can prepare for this type of activity in advance by saving pictures from magazines and catalogues showing a variety of different people. If you get these pictures laminated, they can be used over and over again.

Even if you are not so prepared, you can use pictures from any textbooks you find lying around the classroom. Just bear in mind that you may not be teaching in a room that has suitable textbooks. Languages and humanities rooms will usually provide books with pictures of people, but a science lab may be the only place that gives you the option of diagrams of internal organs.

Once the pupils have their picture of a person, they can provide descriptions, the detail of which will depend upon their ability. They could continue this theme with pair work, questioning each other in the target language about their partner's picture, e.g. 'What colour is his/her hair?' If you have provided them with laminated pictures of famous people, such as pop stars, they could play a type of 'Guess who' by using questions to guess which picture their partner has.

Even if you don't understand the language, it is possible to cover a language lesson effectively.

If you give each pupil pictures of two different people, they could create a conversation between their characters, which they can write in speech bubbles, or as a dialogue. This could range from a very simple conversation involving greeting each other, to more complex topics you suggest. For example, tell them that one of the characters has lost something and is asking the other character for help, or that one character is a tourist and is asking the other for suggestions about what to do and see. Pairs of pupils could then act out the dialogues, or one member of each pair could write out the speeches of one of the characters. Whereas you may not have the language skills to pass comment on the work they prepare, tell them that they could act out their dialogues to the regular teacher on their return.

Collect in any written work at the end of the lesson. If you meet this class again, distribute the work randomly amongst the pupils. Tell them to use dictionaries or their books to mark the work they have been given, correcting any misspelled words. Then redistribute the work again, at random, and select a pupil to read out the work they now have. The original author has to try to identify their own work. For a variation, as a character description is read out, each pupil should sketch what they think the character looks like. These drawings can then be compared for accuracy.

LETTER OR POSTCARD WRITING

This activity can be easily adapted for different ability groups just by adding extra requirements for more advanced pupils. Ask the pupils to write a postcard to their regular teacher or to an imaginary pen friend. They can be sending the postcard from their own locality, or from the last place they went on holiday, or from somewhere that speaks the target language. Younger learners may only know the present tense to express themselves, whereas more sophisticated learners can be asked to use a range of tenses in their work. Once they have planned what they are going to write, give each pupil a rectangle of paper or coloured card onto which they should write their message neatly. Once they have finished the writing, they can provide a picture for the front, even if it's just the name of a place in coloured-in bubble writing.

Letter writing is a variation for more able language learners. Specify who the letter is for: a pen friend, a relation, a hotel, a travel company offering summer jobs, etc. Also tell them the reason they are writing the letter. Simpler letters could be to introduce themselves to a new pen friend. This type of letter would contain information about themselves, their family, their pets, their hobbies and their local area. It could be written entirely in the present tense. For a more demanding task, pupils could write a letter of complaint about a recent imaginary holiday, or an application for a job or university place.

The pupils may need some help in starting their sentences. You should be able to find translations in textbooks, or you could ask one of the language teachers to provide you with translations of the phrases you think you'll need, such as 'Last year I went to ... and saw ...' For any words you don't know, you may be able to refer to a dictionary – if any conscientious pupil has one with them. If you have access to the Internet, the BBC has a comprehensive selection of pages on language learning, including useful phrases and pronunciation sound files in 34 languages. You can access these at www.bbc.co.uk/languages/other/quickfix/index.shtml.

French nouns have two genders: masculine and feminine. Adjectives may change slightly if the noun is feminine. Adjectives such as colours follow the noun. To translate phrases, try the Babelfish translation website: world.altavista.com/tr.

NUMBERS

1–10: un, deux, trois, quatre, cinq, six, sept, huit, neuf, dix.

COLOURS

red	rouge
pink	rose
orange	orange
yellow	jaune
green	vert(e)
blue	bleu(e)
purple	pourpre
brown	brun(e)
white	blanc(he)
black	noir(e)

CLOTHES

trousers	le pantalon (masculine)
jeans	le jean
skirt	la jupe (feminine)
tracksuit	le survêtement
dress	la robe
sweatshirt	le sweatshirt
shirt	la chemise
T-shirt	le T-shirt
blouse	le chemisier

PHRASES FOR GAMES

I went to the shop and I bought ...	Je suis allé au magasin et j'ai acheté ...
My friend's cat is ...	Le chat de mon ami est ...
My friend's dog is ...	Le chien de mon ami est ...
My friend's house is ...	La maison de mon ami est ...

USEFUL WORDS AND PHRASES: FRENCH

German nouns have three genders: masculine, feminine and neutral. Adjectives may change slightly depending on the gender. To translate phrases, try the Babelfish translation website: www.world.altavista.com/tr.

NUMBERS

1–10: eins, zwei, drei, vier, fünf, sechs, sieben, acht, neun, zehn.

COLOURS

red	rot
pink	rosa
blue	blau
green	grün
yellow	gelb
orange	orange
brown	braun
white	weiß
black	schwarz
grey	grau

CLOTHES

trousers	das Hose
jeans	die Jeans
shorts	der Kurzschluß
skirt	der Rock
tracksuit	der Trainingsanzug
dress	das Kleid
sweatshirt	das Sweatshirt
shirt	das Hemd
t-shirt	das T-Shirt
blouse	die Bluse

PHRASES FOR GAMES

I went to the shop and I bought ...	Ich ging zum Geschäft und ich kaufte ...
My friend's cat is ...	Katze meines Freunds ist ...
My friend's dog is ...	Hund meines Freunds ist ...
My friend's house is ...	Haus meines Freunds ist ...

Spanish nouns have two genders: masculine and feminine. Adjectives must agree with the gender of the noun. To translate phrases, try the Babelfish translation website: www.world.altavista.com/tr.

NUMBERS

1–10: uno, dos, tres, cuatro, cinco, seis, siete, ocho, nueve, diez.

COLOURS

black	negro
white	blanco
grey	gris
red	rojo
yellow	amarillo
blue	azul
orange	naranja
pink	rosa
green	verde
brown	marrón
purple	morado

CLOTHES

coat	un abrigo
jacket	una chaqueta
jumper	un suéter
t-shirt	una camiseta
trousers	unos pantalones
shorts	unos pantalones cortos
swimming costume	un traje de baño
socks	unos calcetines
shoes	unos zapatos
trainers	unos deportivos
boots	unas botas
sandals	unas sandalias

PHRASES FOR GAMES

I went to the shop and I bought …	Fui a la tienda y compré …
My friend's cat is …	El gato de mi amigo es …
My friend's dog is …	El perro de mi amigo es …
My friend's house is …	La casa de mi amigo es …

USEFUL WORDS AND PHRASES: SPANISH

Italian nouns have two genders: masculine and feminine. Adjectives may change slightly depending on the gender of the noun. To translate phrases, try the Babelfish translation website: www.world.altavista.com/tr.

USEFUL WORDS AND PHRASES: ITALIAN

NUMBERS

1–10: uno, due, tre, quattro, cinque, sei, sette, otto, nove, dieci.

COLOURS

black	nero
white	bianco
grey	grigio
red	rosso
yellow	giallo
blue	blu
orange	arancione
pink	rosa
green	verde
brown	marrone
purple	viola

CLOTHES

blouse	la camicetta
jacket	la giacca
jumper	il maglione
shirt	la camicia
shoes	le scarpe
skirt	la gonna
tracksuit	il tracksuit
trousers	i pantaloni
T-shirt	la maglietta

PHRASES FOR GAMES

I went to the shop and I bought ...	Sono andato al negozio ed ho comprato ...
My friend's cat is ...	Gatto del mio amico è ...
My friend's dog is ...	Cane del mio amico è ...
My friend's house is ...	Casa del mio amico è ...

Music, drama and art

One thing to remember about music lessons is that they will probably be timetabled in a room full of instruments that will provide much temptation for mischievous fingers so, if you want to emerge without the sound of glockenspiels ringing in your ears, you must make it clear from the start that this lesson is not about playing or fiddling with the instruments! You may well be a talented musician who can rally a class together to rehearse a few popular tunes in harmonious perfection, but if you're not, the ideas here should help you to keep a class focused.

If you don't have any handouts to take in for a music cover lesson, you could resort to any textbooks you chance across in the room. Scour them for diagrams of musical instruments: copying the inside workings of a piano onto plain paper will keep any fast workers occupied once they finish any work you have for them. You may also find biographies of composers, which you can use to make quick quizzes if pupils are starting to drift off task at any point. Another quiz theme could be which section of the orchestra certain instruments belong to. Get the class to do the hard work first by asking teams to write down as many instruments as they can think of that belong to each section: brass, strings, wind and percussion.

The task is to set up their own music store catalogue. Pupils can decide whether their shop is going to specialize in certain instruments, for example electric guitars, or if it will provide a general range. They must feature five instruments in their catalogue. Each instrument should have a description, including what it's made from and the types of music you could use it for. They should also illustrate each description.

If they seem knowledgeable, you can make this more of a challenge by asking pupils to list five instruments that would be used on a certain song that everyone knows, or by a certain composer in his or her work.

If you are in a music room with instruments around the place, let younger pupils choose three to use as a visual focus, and perhaps even choose the best behaved child to play the instrument so that everyone can hear what it sounds like before writing their descriptions. There may be posters on the wall to help.

With minimal advance preparation, you could prepare a photocopiable sheet containing pictures of a variety of musical instruments that they could trace or cut out and stick into their catalogues. Or, as a warm-up activity, provide them with your photocopied pictures and ask them to write down the name of each instrument they can see. For variety, have a selection of pictures that show only part of the instrument.

INSTRUMENT CATALOGUE

Using textbooks (if you find some in the music room), or a resource sheet of information that you provide yourself, read information about four or five composers. The pupils may have been studying a composer already in lessons, so flick through their exercise books to see what they have been doing.

They should choose one composer and make a fact file about them. Give each pupil a sheet of A4 paper, which they can fold in half to make a little booklet. The front is the title page and can be illustrated, the inside two pages should contain details about that composer, and on the back page they can make up their own quiz or create a wordsearch of key words. This way, if they finish the task before the end of the lesson, they can swap booklets to solve each others' quizzes or wordsearches (in pencil), and even peer review their partner's booklet.

If you have nothing prepared, and can find no resources to hand, allow pupils to make up a fact file about their favourite band or musician. Start off by getting teams to create A to Z lists of bands or artists they all know. They can peer mark these lists if you've never heard of half of the names! Another starter would be for them to write down three artists from decades that you specify, although this will only be straightforward for older pupils whose musical tastes are more varied.

INFORMATION ON ELECTRIC GUITARS

www.si.edu/sp/onair/guitar.htm

This site includes a history of the electric guitar and some interesting 'did you know' facts that you could print off and adapt to use in lessons. Some pupils will get excited by electric guitars, especially those aspiring to be rock stars, so if they don't look like the type of kids who will enjoy learning about Mozart, try this instead.

o Read through the information together or in groups and then answer written questions on what they have just learned.

o Make posters to display the information.

o Add details of guitar players they know, and the type of music they play.

AN ENCYCLOPAEDIA OF PERCUSSION

www.cse.ogi.edu/Drum/encyclopedia

There is a different page for each letter of the alphabet.

o You could create a wordsearch using some of the instrument names. Feed the words into a wordsearch maker at www.puzzlemaker.com and your wordsearch is created for you!

o Play a few rounds of a quiz: you give them four instrument names at a time, and they have to guess which one is made up.

o Describe to them one of the more unusual instruments, and ask them to draw what they think it looks like, and how it would work. Then compare their results to the real thing.

o Give them copies of the information and ask them to group together the different instruments according to where in the world they are found. They could label a blank map of the world with picture labels showing where the instruments come from.

PHILHARMONIA ORCHESTRA GUIDE

www.philharmonia.co.uk/thesoundexchange/the_orchestra/sections

This site includes MP3 sound clips of different instruments that you could incorporate into a lesson if you have access to computers. There's a diagram and animated photo of where the sections of the orchestra sit: this could be printed out or displayed on an interactive whiteboard. There are interactive quizzes, a history section and a 'guess what' quiz that you could try if you have computer access. This features sound clips and photos of instruments at strange angles.

ROYAL OPERA HOUSE TEACHER'S PACK ON *CINDERELLA*

info.royaloperahouse.org/Education/Index.cfm?ccs=664

Other resource packs are also available at this site: www.info.royaloperahouse.org/Education/Index.cfm?ccs=436

This is a wonderful resource. You can download the pack as a PDF file from their website. The 34 pages start off with a scene-by-scene description of the story, with photos of the ballet itself. This is followed by numerous well-thought-out activities, aimed at Key Stages 2 and 3, many of which can be done without listening to the music. There is also information on the composer, characters, and even bars of music showing how the music is lively, graceful, etc. You could ask pupils to:

○ suggest modern music that could be played for particular scenes;

○ write a review of the Prince's ball as if they were there;

○ continue the story of Cinderella, and suggest music for the soundtrack;

○ choose another fairy tale, write a summary of what happens and organize the story into scenes. Choose one song to accompany each scene. Think about whether the music would be angry, gentle, romantic, etc.;

○ design costumes and/or make-up for the characters in the ballet. There are photos in the resource to give you ideas.

MUSIC AT SCHOOL
www.musicatschool.co.uk
Resources, quizzes, online lessons and free worksheets to
use with secondary pupils.

DRAMA LESSONS – GENERAL TIPS

Drama lessons can be practical, theoretical or a mixture of both. As a supply teacher, you may well want to stick to the theoretical unless you know the pupils already. However, this might be logistically difficult. The drama lesson might take place in a drama studio, classroom or even the school hall, so be prepared for a lack of chairs and desks. Anticipate distractions that the pupils may try to make the most of while their regular teacher is away, such as a dressing up rail of clothes, screens, props and other equipment.

If there are no desks, ask the pupils to sit in a circle as they come in, so that hopefully their backs will be turned to possible distractions. You may find that they have arrived at the lesson expecting something practical, so don't count on them all having books or even pens. You will need to bring these along or borrow them from another classroom if you intend having written activities.

Once you have established the nature of the group, you might decide they would be better off with written activities. If you choose to have a practical lesson, lay down your rules straight away. Tell them that when you want silence, you will raise your arm in the air. When they see you have your arm raised, they should stand still and quiet, and raise their own arm to show that they have seen. Have a penalty for the last pupil who raises their arm each time, such as stacking the chairs at the end of the lesson. Practical lessons are generally noisy, unless you are studying mime, so probably best avoided if it's an exam period or the classrooms have very thin walls! Split activities into timed sessions to keep the pace of the lesson: three minutes to distribute roles within groups, five minutes to improvise, and so on.

You may find that the class is already studying a play. They may be reading through it, acting it out, or have only just started. Focus on what they already know rather than trying to read through new parts of the play with them. Here are some ideas of activities that can be based on their play. Most of these ideas require copies of the play and a stack of paper.

○ Design the stage set and scenery for a particular scene. Draw and label it on A4 paper.

○ Make a character profile or fact file on two or three of the characters. Based on these details, suggest well-known actors who could take each role in your version of the play.

○ Design costumes and/or make-up for the characters.

○ Make a programme for your production of the play. Include a short summary of what the play is about, some imaginary reviews from theatre critics, biographies of the characters and the actors playing them, and illustrations showing the action on stage at a certain moment.

○ Make a poster advertising tickets for your production of the play. Choose the most suitable image to sum up what the play is about. Add details of where and when it's taking place, and who is starring in it.

○ Design a new book jacket for your copy of the play. Include the same features on your own design, such as pictures, a 'blurb' (the information on the back covers of books) and the title and author.

WORK BASED ON A PLAY

Older pupils may need something more taxing, or you may prefer them to focus on something that will keep them in their seats. If you have time to prepare some printouts, and access to the Internet, the following resources can be adapted to different uses.

Resources on theatre in Ancient Greece, Rome and medieval times can be found on this website: www.tctwebstage.com/ancient.htm. Subsequent pages provide a history of theatre right up to the present day. The information is mostly text, so it's more suited to older pupils.

○ If you make copies or have access to computers to read the information on screen, you could create some detail-finding questions.
○ There are quite a few new or difficult terms in the text, so pupils could highlight the words they don't know and you could create a glossary together.
○ They could use the information to provide a fact file on the theatre in a chosen period, perhaps on eighteenth-century theatre if they are studying a play from that time.

For information about Shakespeare's Globe Theatre, there's an online reference library at www.shakespeares-globe.org/navigation/frameset.htm. You can download a 12-page PDF file containing useful information and pictures.

○ Using the information about the Globe's history and reconstruction, pupils could create their own leaflet guide for visitors to the theatre, perhaps adding any extra information they already know about Shakespeare.
○ They could imagine that it's Tudor times. They have gone to see a production of a Shakespeare play that they have previously studied. Describe what it's like to go to the theatre and what they saw.
○ As a practical variation, this could be done in pairs. One pupil has just seen a play at the original Globe Theatre, and is being interviewed by another pupil outside. They could cover issues such as the atmosphere inside, the seating arrangements and the play itself: which parts the audience seemed to like best, etc.

If you prefer to do something practical with the class, or just want to prevent generating more work that needs marking, try out some of these suggestions.

PRACTICAL DRAMA

o As a warm-up activity, with the pupils in a circle, ask them to tell you their names in turn, followed by which animal they resemble and why. For example, 'I'm like a giraffe because I'm very tall' or 'I'm like a monkey because I'm cheeky and never stop chattering.' A more difficult variation is to compare themselves to a fruit or something less obvious. Or give them a couple of minutes to discuss this with a partner, and then ask them to introduce their partner in this way.

o Other warm-up activities include wink murder and charades. It's probably best not to try anything too physical without knowing the class better or being crystal clear on the school's rules and procedures.

o Read or tell the group a story. It can be a story they already know, such as a fairy tale. Limit the amount of characters, so that they will eventually end up working in small groups. Once they have heard the story, each group has to make up a play based on what they have heard. Give them time to organize themselves, time to rehearse, and then time to perform their version to the rest of the class.

o Read the group a story from a current newspaper, preferably something amusing or exciting rather than the kind of thing that will give them nightmares. Tell them they are eye-witnesses being interviewed for local radio or television, and pairs or groups of three pupils can prepare a short role-play, adding to it imaginatively if they want.

o Follow on from the news interviews by joining two groups together to prepare a television news report on the story, with one or two news readers, an outside correspondent, and one or two eye-witnesses (or similar).

Covering an art lesson can sound like a very easy option. After all, the pupils will have project work to be getting on with, lots of children like art because it means they can sit and chat to their friends while they do something quite therapeutic … don't they? Here's a suggestion: go into the art lesson prepared for a worst-case scenario and then you'll be prepared for anything that could be thrown at you (not literally, let's hope).

Bear in mind that covering a Key Stage 3 class will be quite different to a Key Stage 4 group who have GCSE coursework to get on with. Generally, pupils who are taking art for GCSE will have opted to take it, though this doesn't mean that the whole class will be keen to settle down in a room full of distractions. Art lessons naturally come with great excuses for pupils to get out of their seats and wander around, in order to clean paint brushes or find materials or create a mess by the sink. A Key Stage 3 class might come to the lesson with expectations that this is one of their more fun lessons, with its lack of writing and chances for creativity, so the mood can be buoyant, to say the least.

Think of the essentials before you start this lesson. Is it taking place in a normal classroom, where logistics will help behaviour management, but materials may be located elsewhere? Is it in an art room, with the many distractions of sinks, paints, displays, and a larger space for pupils to mill around? How much time will you need for clearing up, and what strategies will you use to ensure each table or pupil has cleared up their own section? Make it clear at the beginning of the lesson that you will hold each pupil responsible for their own area and explain your penalties for making a mess or distracting others.

You may well not know until the pupils arrive whether they have project work to get on with, but this work may be locked away somewhere that you can't locate straight away, and you'll need something to occupy the pupils for the first part of the lesson. In this case, having a starter prepared to get the class settled when they first arrive is a good idea.

Starters for art lessons can be simple, and easily adapted for other subjects. They will give the pupils something to do straight away, and give you time to settle them and allow for stragglers to arrive. Pupils may arrive expecting to spend ten minutes wandering around the room looking for equipment and project work, but having a starter means you have more control, as they will need to sit at tables straight away.

A quick wordsearch from a grid or a series of anagrams on the board for teams to unravel can be enough to get the majority quiet at the start. Use the names of artists, or colours, or different media such as collage and oil painting.

If you want to prepare an activity in advance, stick pictures of famous paintings onto a sheet of A4 paper, along with a list of the artists' names, or the centuries the paintings are from. Photocopy your master sheet. Pupils can then have a go at matching the artists or centuries to the paintings. A variation would be an 'odd picture out' quiz, where pupils have to identify the picture from the wrong era or movement, or the one that uses a different medium.

One starter that you can stretch out for longer is where you ask for one volunteer to come to the front of the room. Without the other pupils seeing, show them an object that they have to describe to the class without saying what it is. The pupils should draw what the volunteer is describing, and results can be compared at the end. A variation is to have the volunteer feel the object inside a bag, and describe it without seeing the object. You could start this activity off to show the importance of accurate description.

ART LESSON STARTERS

You may decide that the pupils' cries that they have project work to do are not to be entirely trusted, so you may prefer to set them a task yourself. That way, you can check the progress of each pupil in the class and make sure everybody is doing something.

There are plenty of easy options for art lessons that would require only a pencil and some paper: sketch what you can see out of the window, draw a self-portrait or a picture of your partner, draw your own shoe from an unusual angle, draw your own hand, design a new logo for a range of baseball caps.

Add variation or extend the work by asking pupils to produce the picture using different methods: a picture in negative, one that concentrates on shading, a view from the window that changes through the seasons, something done in the style of a particular artist, or a picture using colours to show emotions or feelings.

For Key Stage 3 pupils, here are the units of work suggested for them by the QCA (Qualifications and Curriculum Authority):

Unit 7A	Self-image
Unit 7B	What's in a building?
Unit 7C	Recreating landscapes
Unit 8A	Objects and viewpoints
Unit 8B	Animating art
Unit 8C	Shared view
Unit 9A	Life events
Unit 9B	Change your style
Unit 9C	Personal places, public spaces

More details on each scheme, which may give you further ideas, are available at www.standards.dfes.gov.uk/schemes2/secondary_art

COMIC STRIPS

This activity seems to work particularly well with boisterous boys, so if the class is full of them, give this one a go! If you have time to prepare, find some pictures of superheroes to show them, or print out some of the line drawings from this website on anime and manga art: www.polykarbon.com/tutorials/.

If you have access to computers in the room, pupils could investigate this website, which includes tutorials on how to draw this particular type of cartoon.

Tell them to design their own superhero. They must think of their superhero's particular powers: perhaps elicit a few possibilities from the class and write them up for everyone to choose from. Then they can design a costume for their superhero to change into when he or she turns from their ordinary mild-mannered self.

Once they have designed their superhero, they can create a short adventure in the form of a cartoon strip. Again, if you have time, track down some examples to photocopy and show to pupils, and compare the styles. You could do some formal work analysing the contents and meanings of the cartoon strips: the differences between speech bubbles and thought bubbles, the information boxes, the close-up pictures and how the artist shows action such as fast movement, even the way the clothes move.

If some less-able pupils need more help to create their cartoon strip, provide them with dialogue they have to incorporate into their work, or even write up what should happen in each picture. They then have to decide whether the picture is going to show the action from a distance or a close-up of a face, and make up their own dialogue to put into speech bubbles. This is work that can stretch over more than one lesson.

ART FOR SCHOOLS

www.artforschools.com

This is a commercial site that sells reproductions of art, but the useful thing for your purpose is that its menu comprises the QCA schemes of work, and when you click on each scheme it brings up five or six examples of work by famous artists. You could print these out as examples, or, if you have computers in the teaching room, use them as a starting point for a research project on an artist.

LINKS TO WORTHY WEBSITES

www.devon.gov.uk/dcs/artdesign/websites.htm

Devon County Council's website contains links to art websites and short descriptions of their contents. Find work by famous artists or collected by category, for example African masks. There are also links to sites with tutorials on drawing and painting.

ART INFORMATION SHEETS

ngfl.northumberland.gov.uk/art/default.htm

You can find printable A4 posters here which are information sheets on everything from creating tone to collage, pattern and line drawing. Use them as prompts for pupils' own work, as a focus for the lesson you are covering, or even ask the pupils to use them as a basis for creating their own information sheet about an aspect of art.

ARTY FACTORY

www.artyfactory.com

This website includes tutorials on Egyptian art, pencil portraits, African masks and perspective drawing. Although it is most useful if pupils can access it on a computer, there is so much information on art history and 'how to' sections that it is still useful for printing handouts for the pupils to follow.

LIFE DRAWING

www.wetcanvas.com/ArtSchool/Portraiture/StillLifePortraits/index.html

Lots of written information, which makes it more suitable for older pupils, but you could also use parts of it to direct an art lesson, for example focusing on drawing eyes.

Information technology and business studies

INFORMATION TECHNOLOGY – GENERAL TIPS

IT is taught in various ways in different schools. Some schools prefer to embed it in the rest of the curriculum, whilst others teach it as a distinct subject. The lesson may be timetabled for a computer suite, but you can't guarantee this. Even if the lesson usually takes place in a room full of computers, an enterprising teacher may have taken advantage of the IT teacher's absence to arrange a room swap to access the resources.

Taking a class of pupils in an IT suite presents its own challenges. Many IT suites contain 15 computers, the idea being either that pupils work in pairs, or that there is a rotation system between pupils doing theory and those completing practical work. However, there may be more than 30 pupils in your class; and usually at least one of the computers is out of action. The trick is to use the technology if it is available, but don't rely on it: always have a back-up plan.

Then there is the behaviour of the pupils in the computer room. There are many distractions, from the noise of the printer to squabbling over who gets to use the mouse. Keys are just too tempting not to be tapped and, given the chance, most pupils seem drawn to the noisiest and most unsuitable web pages and programs that the school system will allow them access to.

This is why you have to establish your rules immediately. If the computers are around the edge of the room, make sure the pupils are sitting on their chairs facing the centre of the room where they can't see or fiddle with the computers. This gives you a chance to lay down your rules, and explain how you're going to spend the lesson. Show them your back-up plan of a written activity (or whatever it is), and tell them that anyone not behaving suitably will not be allowed to use the computers, but will do the written work instead.

If the school is new to you and you intend to use the computers, you will need to rely on the pupils to help you pick up the procedures, for example how they log on, whether they have Internet access, what programs are available on the school's network. Make a note of the procedures so you can remember if you work in the school again.

In any group there will be those who are experts at using particular programs, and those who struggle. You could pair up these pupils, or use the knowledgeable pupils as assistant instructors.

The task you set will depend on the age group of the pupils. Tell them you would like them to have produced a word processed piece of work by the end of the lesson that shows they can use various features. Younger pupils could show they know how to change fonts, highlight parts of the text, make headings larger, and include a picture. Some younger pupils, or those with special needs, might seem to take ages just locating the right letters on the keyboard, so reduce the demands for them. You can ask more of the more experienced pupils, such as including numbered lists that have Roman numerals, including a table and page breaks, and so on. Encourage pupils to use the 'Help' facility if they don't know how to do something.

They could either use a piece of work they have completed in another subject as the basis for their word processed piece, or create a page using information on something they are interested in: a fact file on their favourite sport, hobby or music, for example. They might have some homework to do from a previous lesson that would benefit from being word processed.

If you have time, these pieces of work can be printed out and compared, or you could save the printouts to use in another lesson with the same group, or with another group where you want to focus on presentation. Many pupils seem to think that centring their work is the best alignment, and that producing titles using WordArt is necessary, but when you have a batch of papers to compare, they can work out which presentations look best and why.

You can vary this task according to your own strengths and knowledge. More numerate teachers might prefer to work with spreadsheets or even databases. It will depend on what software the pupils have access to. For a lesson based on graphic presentation rather than presenting text, you could use PowerPoint to make slides or Publisher (or other desktop publishing programs) to make anything from newsletters to calendars and business cards.

If the computers have Internet access or there are networked CD-ROMs available you can have a lesson focusing on finding things out. Ask the pupils to pair up, and then tell one of the pair to sit away from the computers and give them something else to do while they wait. The pupils on the computers must visit a website (or the CD-ROM) that you specify and then write out ten or so questions for their partner based on the information found there. If it's a website, tell them to limit their wanderings to just three pages, or the task will be too difficult.

It's then the turn of their partner to access the same website and find the answers to the questions to show they can search for information properly and that they read what they find there: a skill often overlooked by pupils carrying out research projects, as many of them believe that merely printing out the page constitutes doing research!

Alternatively, have both members of the pair on the computer and ask some obscure questions to which they must find the answers as soon as possible. Show them how to access and use search engines, and if you know enough yourself you can explain how to limit searches to UK-based websites, the best ways to input search terms and so on. If you're not an expert in this it doesn't matter: you can use the information retrieval exercise to discover which are the best search terms to use. The BBC's website (www.bbc.co.uk) allows you to search just on the BBC site, which is a good way of preventing any unsuitable websites being accessed by the pupils. Otherwise, Google (www.google.co.uk) is simple to use and extremely comprehensive. Pressing the control key at the same time as the letter 'f' brings up a 'find' box on the screen, and pupils can hunt down information in large amounts of text by using this feature.

To extend this activity, pupils could write a report on the best way to track down information, or produce a 'user guide' for novices. Another idea is to present their findings in a format that you specify, for example a word processed document or PowerPoint presentation.

This task can be carried out using computers, or you could give the pupils copies of a printout from a website. It's an ideal lesson to use if access to computers is limited and you've had time to print out a web page and duplicate it before the lesson.

Ask pupils to compile a report commenting on the various features used on the web page, perhaps giving each a score out of ten. They could comment on the font: is it easy to read? They can consider the use of graphics and pictures, the menus and links, the amount of text, the visual appeal, and so on. This activity can be carried out in pairs or as individuals.

Pupils could write or sketch their ideas for how the page could be improved, including notes on colour schemes that would be suitable and easy to read, and whether there should be music, sound effects or animation. They could comment on how the page might be improved for people who have poor or no vision, or other disabilities.

To extend this task, give them a plain paragraph of information that they must redesign to look like the home page of a website, choosing headings and words to make into clickable links, deciding where images should go, and so on. More able pupils can tie in any other knowledge they have to complete this task: how to make something visually appealing while allowing for slow downloads, how to appeal to different audiences and visitors with one general home page, making navigation easy, etc.

These ideas are for lessons where you can't access computers, and also for when pupils are using computers in rotation and you need something to occupy those not on a computer.

○ Creating information menus. This activity can be carried out on paper. Show the pupils an example (or tell them about one) of how on-screen instructions are often displayed in menus. For example, when you set up a new television or DVD player, information appears on the screen and you have to select and follow the most relevant option. Users need a remote control to scroll up and down or select the number that they want, or there might be touch-screen technology involved. Pupils should have a go at creating a simple menu (or hierarchy) of information that could be displayed on a screen: the subject choice can be yours or theirs. Examples include: creating a menu for tourists to find out about the area; using an ATM; having your picture taken in a photo booth; or ordering a take-away using a screen and remote control. Pupils should draw a diagram showing the main menu choices, and then the further choices resulting from these.

○ Writing a set of instructions. You could tell the pupils that this is a test of their knowledge and powers of explanation. They should write step-by-step instructions for a novice to use a program or complete a task – anything from producing a slide show to shutting down a computer. If there is a computer available you could test their results towards the end of the lesson, with one pupil following one or more sets of instructions.

○ Design a new IT product. Pupils should design a piece of hardware or software that would help them either at school or at home. They can do this individually or in groups. This could lead on to project work that could incorporate some ideas from business studies such as marketing and packaging the product.

REVISE ICT

www.reviseict.co.uk

One teacher's invaluable website, providing professional-looking resources and interactive lessons for pupils.

○ Older pupils can follow the links to BBC news items that feature IT, and then concoct a news round-up, either as a written report or as a five-minute news broadcast.

○ GCSE groups will find the revision section immensely useful. There are past papers, and key concepts and theories are available in a variety of forms, from interactive games to revision notes and quizzes.

○ There are introductory lessons on how to use Word, Publisher, Excel, PowerPoint and Access, so even if you don't know how to work them, you can still use them in the lesson. You could print out the instructions for the pupils to have beside them as they work, although there are also online tasks to complete. These could form the basis of a cover lesson.

MINICLIP

www.miniclip.com

This website has free games and shows. It requires Shockwave for many of the games. It's not educational if you let pupils just play games, but you can use it as a reward at the end of a lesson if they have behaved well enough or have finished their work with ten minutes to spare. You can make it educational, though!

○ Some of the games can be tricky to control, and can help with their co-ordination. You could let them play one of the games for ten minutes, and then ask them to design a new way of controlling the game.

○ If you are rotating the use of the computers, once they have had a turn on a game of their choice, ask them to provide a list of instructions for users.

○ They could write a review of the game, or compare two games.

○ There is a section on 'learning' games. There are word and number games, memory games and puzzles.

WEBSITES TO USE WITH PUPILS

TEACH ICT

www.teach-ict.com

This site contains teaching resources for Key Stage 3, Key Stage 4 and A-level. There are tutorials for software programs and quizzes; and for teachers there are schemes of work to cover the whole of Key Stage 3.

GCSE ICT

www.ictgcse.com

This is another useful site for Key Stage 4 pupils to use: they can work through interactive tutorials, revision guides and quizzes at their own pace. Some of the tasks seem to be text heavy, but the text is written with a GCSE audience very much in mind. There are downloadable exercises, which are given difficulty ratings, and lots of the activities could be suitable for business studies pupils too.

This is often a subject available only to GCSE pupils. The pupils will often have project work they can carry on with independently, but if they don't, here are two ideas for you to lead them through: the first requires computers with Internet access; the second just needs paper and pens.

If you have Internet access, visit this website: 4webgames.com/lemonade. It's a simple simulated business game based on running a lemonade stall. It's American, so it uses dollars for currency. The introduction to the website states: 'You will control all aspects of your Lemonade Stand, from pricing, to quality control, to purchasing your necessary inventory, all while dealing with unpredictable weather, picky customers and inventory wastes. There's also detailed help for most of the screens, to help walk you through some of the decision making process.'

The game is strangely addictive, as you will the customers to buy your lemonade and groan when all your ice melts! If the pupils can tear themselves away, they should write a report on what happened during the simulation, the factors that affected sales (such as the weather and price) and how they could have improved their profit. More able pupils could have a go at creating an idea for their own simulation to be made into a simple game, coming up with their own business idea and writing out the variables that could affect it. There are other simulation games available at the same website.

The class might have been introduced to doing a SWOT analysis, which is assessing a business opportunity for Strengths, Weaknesses, Opportunities and Threats. This is something a class can do without computers. Give them an idea or ask them to come up with their own business plan, and then perform a SWOT analysis on it. They could work in groups, drawing up tables or reports, and then make presentations to the rest of the class. Each group could have a different business idea, or you could ask them all to analyse the same one. For example, they might each be given an imaginary stall at the school fete, with one selling cakes, another selling bric-a-brac, a tombola, etc.

If you want more business studies lesson plans, take a look at www.thetimes100.co.uk/teachers/lessons.php. There are case studies and downloadable lesson plans.

Humanities

Schools teach and timetable humanities in various ways. In some schools geography, history and religious education (RE, or RS for religious studies) are taught separately from Year 7. Other schools may teach combined humanities, at least for Year 7, and the humanities department may work closely together on schemes of work. In Key Stage 4, humanities subjects offer a lot of options: GCSEs in combined humanities, RE short courses, travel and tourism GNVQs and leisure and tourism in addition to geography, and so on. Sometimes Key Stage 3 classes learn all three subjects all year round, and in some schools they teach in groups rotating the subjects, studying geography for one term and then history for the next.

The suggestions here treat the humanities as three distinct areas: geography, history and RE. Where possible, the ideas are for stand-alone lessons that will probably cover topics that the pupils have previously encountered. This is so that as a supply teacher you are not introducing new areas of study, but relying on a general understanding that the pupils probably first encountered in primary school.

There are so many topic areas that can be covered in humanities lessons that if you have a particular area of interest yourself, you can usually adapt it in different ways and for different year groups. For single lessons you can use a photocopied page from a library book and base a series of questions on it; even if these are comprehension questions, the pupils are still learning something about the topic and using skills like skimming and scanning texts for information, which are important skills to have right across the curriculum.

If you are working with a page of information from the Internet or photocopied from a library book, or even a page from a *Horrible Histories* book you have lying around at home, there are several activities and outcomes you can do across the humanities subject range, even if it's a subject not explicitly mentioned here, such as classical civilization. Each subject will have particular skills taught by the regular teachers, but as a supply teacher you wouldn't be expected to intentionally include these in your lessons. As a result, these lessons may seem weighted towards factual knowledge rather than being skills-based.

Distribute your photocopies and read the text and study any diagrams together. Ask the pupils to make up five or ten quiz questions, along with the answers, on what they have just read. Choose one pupil to read out their first question. They can choose someone to answer it, or you could work your way around the classroom. If the pupil answers the question correctly, it's their turn to direct a question at somebody else. This tests whether they have absorbed the information they have just read.

After reading a chunk of text, there may be words or concepts that are new or long forgotten. Pupils can try to work out their meanings from context, or from dictionaries. They can then form their own definitions. Choose the most lucid definition to write up on the board, and have everybody copy it down.

Another way of checking understanding is to ask the pupils to present the information in a different format. This could be for a different audience, which is a way of ensuring that they use their own words rather than simply copy what's already there. They could present the information as:

○ an information poster;
○ a leaflet that persuades somebody to do something (for example litter recycling in geography or giving women the vote in history);
○ a textbook page for a younger year group;
○ a speech;

o a letter (especially good in history, e.g. pretend you are Queen Victoria writing to Parliament about an issue);

o a fact file or biography.

While the pupils are getting settled at the beginning of the lesson, have an activity for them to do straight away. This gives you the opportunity to discover if any work has been set, and also to leaf through their exercise books to discover the topic they are currently studying.

For history, muddle up a series of dates on the board for them to put into chronological order: include AD and BC dates to make it tougher. If one pupil finishes quickly, invite them up to write out the next muddled up series.

For any of the humanities subjects, ask them to read over their work or notes from the previous lesson, then to create three or five questions based on their work to ask the rest of the class. Let them take it in turns to ask their questions. This has the advantage of giving you an insight into what they've been studying.

You could choose some obvious key vocabulary, however loosely connected with the subject, and write it up in anagrams on the board for them to solve. Again, if there are high fliers who finish quickly, get them doing the work and generating some new anagrams for you!

With key vocabulary you can ask them to create crossword-style clues for each word. If there is slack time at the end of the lesson, they can use the vocabulary to create real crosswords. It helps to have graph paper for activities like this. Lower abilities can make up wordsearches from the key words; just tell them to pay extra special attention to the spellings or the wordsearches may never be solved!

This activity can turn into project work if you meet the same class for more than one lesson. Individuals, pairs or groups should plan a tour of either local or national attractions for a group of visiting tourists.

You can allocate a particular type of tourist to each group/individual, or randomly generate them by writing up five or six types on the board, for example: a group of teenagers on a language course; middle-aged Americans; Australian backpackers; families from Europe. Ask each group to choose a number between one and five, and then randomly write the numbers next to each tourist type for the groups to find out which type they must cater for.

The outcome for this lesson can be a written report, a poster advertising the tour, a brochure entry, or more comprehensive project work if the theme continues over several lessons. You will need to provide details such as how long the tour should last, forms of transportation to be used, maximum distances that can be travelled each day, and either the types of attractions the groups want to visit or the names of specific places. Older pupils might work out for themselves what attractions would appeal to particular groups of tourists.

If you have atlases or maps to hand, pupils can work out the distances and routes of the tour. If not, they can concentrate on choosing suitable places for the tour to visit, and work out a sensible itinerary. You could specify that they should include, for example, a seaside resort, a theme park, an ancient monument, a castle and a city. Pupils can either use their own knowledge or maps to help them locate suitable places.

Once they have produced an itinerary there are more challenges you can throw into the mix. Tell them that a particular road is closed for repairs and that they must redesign their routes accordingly. Add a tourist to their imaginary tour group who has particular needs that must be taken into consideration. Tell them the theme park is closed and they must find an alternative in the locality. Another variable that can be changed is the time of year the tour will take place: for example, an hour on the beach is less attractive in winter than in summer, so they need to choose a resort that also has undercover attractions.

During this lesson, pupils can design their own symbols for a weather map. To start with, ask pupils to come up with lists of the types of weather whose symbols we see most frequently, and then the symbols that represent the different weather scenarios. Ask them to differentiate further: describe five or more different types of rain, for example, from drizzles to sudden heavy downpours.

You could categorize the types of weather in different ways: weather according to seasons, British and non-British weather; they could think of positive and negative aspects of different types of weather, such as sunburn and hosepipe bans or flooding and drowning crops. Small groups of pupils could make displays about particular types of weather, including creating new symbols for a weather forecast, or they could work individually to design new symbols for a variety of weather.

If the classroom has access to computers, you could use the BBC's weather website at www.bbc.co.uk/weather. Enter a place name to get a local five-day forecast, look at satellite charts, investigate climate change and the pollen index. There's even a section called 'Painting the weather' where you can select a weather symbol and the site returns works of art depicting the chosen weather – a useful addition to groups that are making displays on weather types.

Low-ability sets could have a go at painting the weather themselves; they divide a piece of paper into four boxes, and draw a different type of weather in each box. When they have finished this, you can make it into a game. Write up some vocabulary associated with different types of weather, for example: clouds, lightning, wind force, gales. Pupils should copy the correct words into the four different pictures they've produced, which will obviously depend on the types of weather they've chosen to illustrate. The first pupil to match ten or so words to their pictures correctly is declared the winner.

Although maps are only one aspect of geography, they are versatile enough to be used a number of ways in lessons. If you regularly work in the same area, print some copies of the locality map from the Ordnance Survey website (www.ordnancesurvey.co.uk) and laminate them so they can be used over again. Pupils can use board pens to mark laminated maps, and then wipe the ink away at the end of the lesson.

Maps can be used for starter activities. One idea is a treasure hunt with clues. Give the pupils coordinates for their starting place, then read out instructions using named roads, features or compass bearings. Pupils trace the route you describe and when they arrive at the correct destination, tell them to take a certain letter of the place name to be the first letter of their clue. Repeat this until they have their key word, which could be a clue to the location of some mythical buried treasure. You could use the school's reward system for the first pupils to locate the 'treasure', or if the lesson is just before a break, the winners can be the first allowed to leave. You could allow the winners to finish the lesson with their own treasure hunt for the rest of the class to follow.

If you have no maps to hand, you can still include the topic in the lesson. Ask the pupils to draw the map of the route they take to school: this sounds easy, but can actually be quite tricky if it involves a long journey. If they live just round the corner, then they can produce a map of the journey to the nearest shopping centre or local attraction instead.

On a smaller scale, they could draw a map of the school that shows it in its location, or you could hand out photocopies of a plan of the school and ask them to expand the map to include local roads and features.

MAP ZONE

www.mapzone.co.uk

This is an animated (and noisy) website designed for children, with games, competitions and homework help. There are useful sections you could use with a class in a room with computers, including explanations and interactive exercises on contours, compass bearings, symbols and grid references. Games include jigsaw puzzles on parts of the UK and a flags of Europe game. There's enough here to keep a Key Stage 3 class busy for at least one lesson.

ORDNANCE SURVEY

www.ordnancesurvey.co.uk

Enter a place name and this website will retrieve the OS map and display it on screen. If you use the map on screen, you can zoom in and out, and navigate with the 8-point compass. Otherwise, choose the print option and use copies to do some map work with the class. Historical maps are also available here.

GEOINTERACTIVE

www.geointeractive.co.uk

Interactive resources for geography teachers. There are over 500 free resources available, and also a subscription section including puzzles, tutorials, PowerPoint presentations and worksheets. Highly recommended for handy worksheets.

GEOGRAPHICAL ASSOCIATION

www.geography.org.uk

Downloadable teaching resources, including ideas for starters and plenaries.

GEOGRAPHY IN THE NEWS

www.geographyinthenews.rgs.org

A site from the Royal Geographical Society that is especially useful for GCSE lessons. There are case studies on recent events and issues, such as erupting volcanoes and earthquakes. After each article there are teaching ideas suitable for Key Stage 3, Key Stage 4 and A-level.

USEFUL WEBSITES FOR GEOGRAPHY

LOCAL HERITAGE INITIATIVE
www.lhi.org.uk/teachers/geography/index.html
Geography activity sheets to download as PDFs or Word
files, and an image gallery.

OUTLINE MAPS
www.eduplace.com/ss/maps/
Outline maps (PDFs) to print off for classroom use.
Choose between maps with or without labels. Use them
to add physical features like rivers or to label capital
cities.

NATIONS ONLINE PROJECT
www.nationsonline.org
A guide to the countries and nations of the world, this
website is a useful starting place if you want to base a
lesson on a particular country. Lots of useful
information, such as population figures, maps, flags,
currencies, A–Z country fact files with useful links to
find out more.

In history, Key Stage 3 pupils generally learn about Britain and the wider world from the Norman Conquest right up to the World Wars of the twentieth century. Schools choose their own emphases, and also their own options in addition to the core requirements. In primary schools, pupils have usually studied the Romans, Vikings, Anglo-Saxons, Celts, Ancient Egyptians and so on. At GCSE the topic areas vary enormously. Therefore it can be difficult to second guess what any particular group is doing.

One way around this is to come prepared with something photocopiable from a popular topic area, like the Ancient Egyptians. Make sure it has plenty of juicy facts for pupils to enjoy, but the facts can be about anything from toys to burial practices. The outcome of this lesson is for pupils to make their own 'Horrible Histories' booklet from a piece of paper folded in half to make a booklet shape, with a front cover and two or three pages of information inside. The name 'Horrible Histories' is from the books by Terry Deary, which feature interesting and off-beat facts in cartoon form. You don't have to concentrate on the horrible parts of history unless you want to!

Once you have read through the information together, the pupils should choose a number of facts to include in their booklet. Each fact must be rewritten in their own words, and accompanied by a cartoon or picture. You could put a choice of questions on the board to focus their investigation, such as 'What did the Egyptians believe would happen to them in the afterlife?' or 'What was it like to be a child in Ancient Egypt?'

If you see the same class more than once then this can be continued over more than one lesson. It can even be done without any preparation by you: they could use the topics they are currently studying in history, reading through their exercise books or textbooks to scour for details, and then turning the information into a booklet. Key Stage 4 pupils will probably welcome the light relief that such a lesson brings, but if they demand something more serious, leave out the cartoons and tell them they are making a revision booklet of key facts from their current topic of study.

Every secondary pupil should know how to construct a timeline. Of course, there are always exceptions to this rule, so you could ask groups of pupils to create a set of guidelines on how to make a timeline before you move on to the main activity of the lesson. This is also useful because it gives you some time to flick through a few of their exercise books and see what topics they have been studying. Look for something that particularly mentions a lot of dates, whether these are across years or on a shorter timescale of days within a year.

When you have established with the class how a timeline should be done, give each pair of pupils or individuals the largest piece of paper you can find. Ask them to turn in their exercise books to the work they did on the topic you saw earlier. It's probably easier to ask them to work in pairs for this, in case some of the pupils were absent or don't have their books.

Their task is to construct a timeline about the event or topic they have been studying. Give them large sheets of paper so there is plenty of room around the edge of the timeline for when they have finished stage one, which is to draw the line, section off the time segments, label the dates, and put on the key events.

In stage two they choose about three events to add in detail to their timeline. They can choose how they wish to do this. They could write a summary of the event next to the labelled date on their timeline. They could draw a portrait of one of the people involved in the event, or a map of where the event took place. They could even create newspaper-style headlines and summaries about each event, or write out the script of a news broadcast. The finished result should be that each pupil or pair has created a timeline correctly labelled and decorated with pictures or furnished with extra details.

MINI-PROJECT

This activity is more suited to lower school pupils, and also those of low ability. It can be carried on over more than one lesson, or if you prefer to instil a sense of urgency you can impose a time limit and finish by the end of the lesson. Establish what topic the class is currently studying, and then give them a choice of mini-project to do that is based on that topic. The themes could include Homes, Fashions, Social Groups, Food and Drink or Famous Characters.

You might be limited to the notes they have in their exercise books, but if there are textbooks or library books that can also be used, so much the better. If there are Internet-ready computers in the classroom, allocate each pupil some time to do extra research: the BBC's history website is a good starting place and covers just about all the historical periods taught in schools. It's at www.bbc.co.uk/history.

Most groups will need some guidance with what to include in their project. For Homes they could include plans and descriptions of a range of homes from the time, whether castles or roundhouses, merchants' houses or villas. If this project is continued over several lessons, they could find out about furniture and decoration, as well as the technology (or lack of it) to light and heat the house. They might include charts to compare the housing of different groups or classes of people, or even include a mock estate agents poster for one of the houses. For the Fashions project they could draw the clothing, compare what was available for different social classes, investigate the manufacturing process or trade routes, find out about make-up and wigs, and design a fashion catalogue or clothing display for a shop window. A project on Food and Drink could investigate the crockery, cutlery and cooking implements of the period, or involve writing a menu for an inn or restaurant of the time.

USEFUL HISTORY WEBSITES

SCHOOL HISTORY

www.schoolhistory.co.uk

There are over 600 freely downloadable worksheets here, as well as resources to use in the lesson, if you have computers or an interactive whiteboard. There's also a teachers' forum (discussion board) full of helpful suggestions and links.

LEARN HISTORY

www.learnhistory.org.uk

This website has free history resources and is particularly useful for its collection of links.

PASSMORES SCHOOL HISTORY WEBSITE

passmoreshistory.homestead.com/home.html

An invaluable site, especially if you have a series of history lessons to cover. There are plans for each lesson in units of work, handouts and homework sheets to print out, differentiated work for special needs pupils, and even resources such as sequencing cards, grids and charts to download and print.

GCSE HISTORY PAGES

www.historygcse.org

Especially for pupils following the Schools History Project course, this website contains homework help and revision guides, so it could be used with a GCSE group if you have access to computers.

ACTIVE HISTORY

www.activehistory.co.uk/sample_activities.htm

This is mostly a subscription-based website, although it does contain a sample of free resources for teachers. There is a series of handouts and worksheets on Jack the Ripper – not for the fainthearted, but a useful scheme of work to follow if the pupils need to work on looking at sources.

SPARTACUS EDUCATIONAL

www.spartacus.schoolnet.co.uk

This site contains a wealth of information sorted into topics, so will probably be of most use if you are taking a class for the second time and know which topic they are covering. It includes a virtual school with links to online lessons and resources, again sorted into topic areas.

Other history teaching websites that contain downloadable worksheets, images, revision help and links to useful resources can be found at:

HISTORY MAD
www.historymad.com

SCHOOLS HISTORY – TEACHER RESOURCES
www.schoolshistory.org.uk/teachersresources.htm

GCSE MODERN WORLD HISTORY REVISION SITE
www.johndclare.net

HISTORY ON THE NET
www.historyonthenet.com

If you are covering religious education or religious studies, it can be difficult to know what to expect. All Key Stage 3 pupils have RE lessons, and at Key Stage 4 pupils may have general RE not leading to an exam, GCSE RE, or they might be taking a GCSE short course. The school will have chosen a curriculum to follow, but RE may also be used as a time to learn about and debate ethical issues. Some advice to bear in mind when debating ethical issues is that the class will be a lot quieter if they settle down to written work, so if you are brave enough to tackle a debatable issue then have a written task ready to restore order.

Be careful if you are supply teaching in a religious school, as they will have particular emphases for their RE lessons.

It's worth having some lesson ideas in mind that are built around themes rather than specific religions, which will allow you to incorporate the topic currently being studied, whether that is information about a particular religion or ethics debates. Themes could include Food and Feasting, Celebrations of Spring, Rites of Passage (all of which are elaborated on in this section), Religious Buildings and Places, Life after Death, Rules and Commandments, Creation Stories, Festivals, Religious Leaders and Founders, Religion and War, Religious Symbols.

On the other hand, you may find that the class has been studying the story of Buddha or the five pillars of Islam, in which case you can create an activity that reinforces their knowledge without moving them beyond their current topic. Ask them to present the information in a different way, such as a letter, newspaper article, poster, textbook page for younger pupils, etc.

This could be a theme for a lesson or series of lessons when you don't know in advance what the class has been studying. Ask for examples of when we have special meals and foods, such as Sunday lunch or Christmas dinner or birthday cakes. You'll get lots of examples to use in multi-cultural classes. Ask the pupils what it means to share a meal and eat together; you could even have class surveys on how often pupils sit at a table to eat, how often the whole family is there, who does the cooking, and so on.

Leaf through their exercise books to find out if the class has been studying a particular religion, and then ask them for examples they have learnt so far about feasting in that religion. This could be Passover meals, Eids, etc. Find out if any food is banned, and the reason for this. Written outcomes could include a menu for a special occasion, descriptions of a religious feast, a chart showing the origins of celebrations or a comparison between different religions. If there are textbooks in the teaching room, encourage pupils to use them to investigate the topic further.

If you want a more issue-based lesson for a GCSE class, move on to consider the role of food in our society, and the famines in other parts of the world. What would be the consequences of everyone in Britain giving up meat for 40 days? Or permanently? How would this affect the farming industry or even the fashion industry? What if we had no supermarkets? What if we had food rationing? Pupils could gather ideas for a debate, or if they need quietening down they could write a report or discursive essay.

FOOD AND FEASTING

CELEBRATIONS OF SPRING

This is a theme for a lesson that could develop into project work. You can adapt this idea to fit in with other times of year, such as All Souls/Hallowe'en, winter, midsummer or harvest time.

Prepare some examples of how different religions celebrate the coming of spring, e.g. Tu B'Shvat in Judaism and the pagan origins of Easter rituals, or elicit these from the class if they are older and wiser! Ask the pupils to list the hopes and worries people in the past (especially agricultural societies) may have had about spring, and how and why these differ today. You can tie this in to a particular religion they are studying, especially if there are textbooks to hand that you can flick through while they are completing introductory tasks.

Ask them for ways in which we could mark the coming of spring in today's society, such as practical ideas that have environmental benefits. Lower abilities can present their findings by drawing a card or calendar to celebrate spring or show a particular religion's celebrations.

Build up a chart comparing the different ways religions celebrate spring, and find points of comparison. Higher-ability groups can use this to produce a piece of written work.

A variation on this would be to look up current religious festivals taking place and use them as a theme for the lesson. You can find a multi-faith calendar at www.bbc.co.uk/religion/interactive/calendar/index.shtml.

For a straightforward lesson with individual work, print out some information or a worksheet from the Internet and set questions for pupils to show they have understood what they have read and that they can locate information. Extension tasks can be creative work based on what they have learned.

This themed lesson allows you either to incorporate what the class have already learned, or to run a lesson with no background knowledge at all. Explain that rites of passage are special things that happen to us when we reach certain stages in life. These may be religious, such as baptism, or not religious, like receiving the key to the door at the age of 18 or 21. Lower abilities might feel more comfortable using a term like 'path of life' instead.

Ask pupils to draw a timeline for a person's life, and mark off all the rites of passage they can think of. With older or more able pupils, ask them to add any religious rites of passage they know of. Try to categorize the rituals: those to do with birth and new life; those concerned with growing up and reaching adulthood; others to do with marriage and childbirth; and those concerning old age and finally death.

You could carry out surveys among the class to find out which rituals they have heard of, and any rituals that have happened to them such as baptisms or bar mitzvahs. Ask them to display the results in different ways. If you have Internet access or textbooks to hand, ask pupils to research a particular rite of passage or all of those belonging to one religion. They could design clothes to be worn at a ceremony, draw up invitations or programmes, create a menu of food for the special occasion, or even invent their own rite of passage for a special time of life.

RITES OF PASSAGE

BBC RELIGIONS
www.bbc.co.uk/religion/religions
A vast resource, detailing 14 religions and including world-wide statistics. You can find links to topics for ethics too.

RE ONLINE
www.reonline.org.uk
A substantial website with teacher and student sections. There's a handy calendar of festivals so you can keep your lessons topical.

RELIGIOUS STUDIES
www.religiousstudies.co.uk
One dedicated teacher's contribution to the Internet. IT resources such as PowerPoint presentations you could use in lessons, as well as schemes of work, revision guides for pupils, worksheets from Key Stage 3 to A-level, and even support for A-level philosophy.

RE:QUEST
www.request.org.uk/teachers/info/teachers.htm
Lots of information and downloadable resources on Christianity.

CHIGWELL SCHOOL'S RE DEPARTMENT
www.chigwell-school.org/academic/departments/rs/siteadmin/index.html
Useful links to further information on world religions. You can also download course booklets for GCSE topics.

THORPE ST ANDREW SCHOOL RELIGION
www.tsas-re.freeserve.co.uk
This school's website is very clearly set out with hundreds of useful links.

THE BIG MYTH
mythicjourneys.org/bigmyth
An animated site that lets you explore creation myths from around the world. It uses sound and appealing animations, and there are follow-up exercises.

RELIGION FOR SCHOOLS
www.world-faiths.com
There are pages for each of the major world religions, and resources for teachers to download.

Design and technology

DESIGN AND TECHNOLOGY – GENERAL TIPS

Having a D&T lesson to cover can mean one of several areas: food, resistant materials, textiles and so on. GCSE groups may also take graphics, systems and control, engineering or electronics; they will probably have coursework projects to do.

At Key Stage 3, the class may be in the middle of a project and you will probably be in a specialist teaching room with distractions such as taps, sinks, ovens, tools and dangerous-looking cutting machinery. Unless you are experienced in teaching D&T, inform the class straight away that this will not be a practical session as their usual teacher is away. There are too many health and safety issues for a supply teacher to be expected to deal with. Instead, choose something for them to do that allows them to express their practical abilities, but that involves every pupil sitting in their seat rather than wandering the room fiddling with equipment.

An advantage to covering this type of lesson is that teaching groups are often smaller than for many other subjects, so the pupils are easier to keep an eye on. Also, you can take inspiration from whatever you have on you, from the chocolate wrapper in your lunch box to the design of your bag.

The bad news is that many schools allocate double periods for D&T, which means that you have to find something to do for a much longer period than for other subjects. You can help to fill the time by having a long starter activity or stopping at the end of the first period for a quiz, whether subject-related or general knowledge. For quizzes, get the pupils to do the work for you by asking small groups to write sets of questions along with the answers and then using a mixture of questions from every group. This way, if you don't know much about sport or pop music you don't need to worry because the pupils have done the work for you!

You could decide to run two tasks during the time to stop the pupils getting bored and therefore potentially more disruptive towards the end of the double period, or add pace to the lesson by stopping them every 15 to 20 minutes and asking for feedback on what they've done so far, or for some quick-fire questions.

There are some general starter activities you could do for design and technology lessons. Ask pupils to write down the five most important safety rules about the room they are in (if it's a practical room) or about participating in their usual food technology, textiles or resistant materials lesson. Once they have individual lists, put the pupils into groups and ask them to come up with one definitive list, which they can then share with the class.

If there are vocabulary lists on the walls or in their books, write up a few anagrams of key words on the board for them to decipher as they come into the room and settle down, or provide them with crossword-style clues to the words. Once they are settled, you could play Hangman to elicit key words. Harder still, ask them to make a D&T alphabet: they should write the letters A to Z down the margin of their page and think of subject-appropriate words to start with each letter.

For something a bit different, and if you have time to prepare, take a look at this American website on food: www.foodtimeline.org/food2a.html. It's a series of links, so you can discover how the Ancient Maya used corn or how to balance a Navajo diet; or follow links to British sites to find out about rationing in 1945 or medieval feasts. There are links to information on food diversity, such as breakfasts around the world and Japanese or Mexican traditions. Use the information to give the pupils something to read, and then quiz them on it. If it's a food technology lesson, you could use the information to provide a theme for the whole lesson. There's a section on food packaging that you could use if the D&T lesson is on resistant materials, as this could then lead on to designing packaging for different foodstuffs.

FOOD TECHNOLOGY:
YOU ARE WHAT YOU EAT

Instruct the pupils to list what they had to eat over the past few days or week. They should include all snacks and sweets as well as what they ate at mealtimes. They can also include the drinks they had, from water to coffee to cola. Once they have this data you can use it in several ways.

More able or older groups should try sorting their food diaries into food groups:

o breads, cereal, rice and pasta;
o fats, oils and sweets;
o fruits and vegetables;
o protein (meat, poultry, fish, beans, eggs and nuts);
o dairy (milk, yoghurt and cheese).

They can then represent their personal findings in chart form to show how many servings they had of each food group over the period. Serving sizes are approximately a cupful. You don't need to comment on their findings, but instead leave it to them to comment on their own charts, using what they have already learnt in food technology. There might be a food pyramid poster in the room if you're teaching in the subject room, and you can direct them to that to compare their diet with a suggested healthy diet.

Another use for this data is for them to compare their findings in groups and construct a bar chart for their group, or produce a questionnaire to interview other class members about their eating choices and produce a report. Younger pupils could draw an outline of a person and try to represent what they ate by drawing the foodstuffs inside the figure.

To extend the task, pupils can write a report on how their diet could become healthier: what do they need to eat less of, and what do they need more of, and why? If being objective about their own diet is difficult, swap the findings around the class and ask them to critique an anonymous set of findings from someone else in the class.

Write lists of foods up on the board. For younger pupils, this can be ready-made or prepared food, for example lasagne, boiled potatoes, pork chops, apple pie, and so on. For older or more able pupils, the lists should be of ingredients, such as pasta sheets, milk, onions, apples, pastry, etc.

Once you have substantial lists, tell the class that they must each create a menu for different situations or different types of people. For example: a healthy packed lunch to take to school; an Italian-themed dinner; a balanced hot meal for a vegetarian. They can use only the ingredients or foodstuffs on the board.

To make this more difficult, ask each pupil to choose ten numbers between one and however many items you have on the board. Once they have written down their ten numbers, randomly allocate sequential numbers, starting with one, to the items listed on the board. Tell them to find the food items with the numbers they chose, and ask them to create a meal or menu from their random ingredients.

You can ask pupils to create menus without providing food lists. Again, you will need to provide them with scenarios, for example lunch for somebody who is allergic to dairy products, or a family dinner.

This is a good task for keeping classes occupied during long lessons as they can spend a while on the presentation of their menus, making sure the presentation fits the theme of the scenario. They could even invent their own restaurant and design logos and themes for their menus.

CREATING MENUS

TEXTILES: FABRIC DESIGN

For a textiles lesson that requires no technical expertise from you, creating a fabric design just requires paper and pencils for the pupils to sketch out their designs. Give them an idea of what they are designing the fabric for. One idea is a series of children's soft toys: a cuddly toy zoo or farm, for example. They should choose five animals that will be made into soft toys, and then design the fabric that will be used in their manufacture. Patterns for cows, for example, will require more detail than patterns for animals with solid blocks of colour, but they should also think of places where the colour will vary, such as on hooves and heads. To extend this task, more able pupils could have a go at designing the pattern for one of the animals, which would be cut out and made into the soft toy.

Another idea is to design a fabric that could be used to cover their school planners or diaries. They could choose a theme, such as making the cover look like a type of jacket (it is a book jacket, after all!), for example a denim jacket or a tuxedo. The advantage of this is that designing the pattern (or outline) of a book shape is quite easy. More able pupils can think how they would attach the material to their planners, and decide on how much of the inside covers would be covered up by material too, including the implications of this: would they be able to shut the planner properly? They could think of ways to distinguish their planner from the others: having studs or sequins spelling out their name, for example.

With activities like this, if the class has finished with ten or fifteen minutes to spare, arrange all the designs on the desks and allow the pupils to move around looking at the different designs. They could even award points to each design on criteria that you give them or that they decide upon, such as originality, practicality, neatness, etc.

If you have time to print off some information from the Internet, there are many websites out there with a textiles theme which you can use in a number of ways in textiles lessons. The advantage of this is that it can lead on to project work: useful if you cover the same group more than once. Use the information to make up quizzes, ask the pupils to create information leaflets using the facts and ideas, or find templates to use for designs.

QUILT ETHNIC

www.quiltethnic.com/lessonplans.html
At this website you'll find some fascinating links, some of which are to ready-made lesson plans. Older pupils can learn about the significance of African painted and dyed cloth and have a go at designing their own fabric in the same style. They can read about how textiles can convey meanings using pattern and colour. There are also links to information about Native American blanket and quilt design.

THEME PARK DESIGN

teacher.scholastic.com/lessonplans/unit_themeparkdesign _lesson1.htm
This is a detailed lesson plan for a large D&T project, but you can just concentrate on the textiles element. It leads up to designing costumes for the characters at a theme park.

NO FRILLS NEEDLEWORK RESOURCES

www.needlework.com/resourcespage/nofrillsrsrc.html
Find links to museums and galleries, designers, needlework designs and design inspiration.

BOYS WHO SEW

www.craftscouncil.org.uk/boyswhosew
A useful website if you're in an all-boys school, or in a class with a large number of boys. There is a slide show of the artists' work along with information about them.

TEXTILES ONLINE

www.e4s.org.uk/textilesonline/index.htm
This is a useful website to use if you are in a room with computers that the pupils can access. There's all sorts of information about the textiles industry as well as details

about environmental concerns. To use the interactive
activities the computers will need Shockwave.

COSTUMES IN TIME

www.princetonol.com/groups/iad/lessons/middle/dance.
htm#Costume

Links to collections of historical costumes. Pupils with
access to computers could use this as a starting point to
research fashion throughout history. For example, follow
the link to the Renaissance Tailor to find patterns,
Elizabethan sewing tips and images of costumes. You
could provide a theme for the research, telling the pupils
to investigate the costumes they would dress characters
in for a production of a play or musical that you specify
or that they choose.

For this aspect of D&T, pupils have to understand materials. This is taken from the government's Standards Site (www.standards.dfes.gov.uk) and shows what pupils in Year 7 should be able to do:

○ classify materials by their properties and sources, e.g. hard/soft, ferrous/non-ferrous metal, thermoplastic/thermosetting plastic;
○ consider basic surface finishes, e.g. edge polishing acrylic, sealing wood, primer, undercoat and gloss paint on mild steel;
○ consider physical properties, e.g. the grain of wood, brittleness of acrylic, elasticity of PVC, malleability of aluminium;
○ become aware how the extraction, use and eventual disposal of some materials affect the natural environment.

You could set the class a single lesson investigation using these criteria on whatever you have to hand. They could even use the contents of their pencil cases! Ask pupils to draw tables with sections for each of the four bullet points above. They should then fill in their table with information about their chosen object. Information about some of these areas will be quite limited without knowledgeable instruction, and so they could use the investigation just as a starting point.

Once they have completed a chart detailing what they know about the object(s) chosen, they can then start to design new objects using different materials. For example, how could a common old pencil be improved? Would making it wider make it slightly easier to hold? What about rubber grips to make it more comfortable? How could you protect the rubber on the end? What about designing a 'Swiss army'-style pencil case that stops you losing the contents? Ask them to draw and label their new designs.

The beauty of a task like this is that you can use whatever is to hand, such as packed lunches, chocolate bar wrappers, storage jars and boxes that you find in the D&T room or in their own school bags.

The emphasis for this project for the non-specialist has to be on the design rather than the technology! The aim is for the pupils to design on paper a robot to carry out a specific task. You could set them a task for a robot to do: picking apples, carrying their school books around for them, washing up, cleaning a bike, etc. Or they could choose their own use for a robot.

The first stage is to note down what the chosen task will require of a robot. For example, an apple-picking robot will need to stretch to reach up into the trees. How could it do that? Having a telescopic body might be one idea. It also needs to grip the apples, but not too hard or it might bruise them. The robot will be working outside so they will have to design a shell to stop water or the elements affecting its mechanisms and electronics.

Once they have the list of criteria, pupils can draw their design on paper. The degree to which it is labelled will depend on their age and ability. They could choose two or three of the robot's features to show in a large detailed drawing, illustrating how the mechanism would work, or focusing on the technical element: for example, how a gripping hand would work.

If there is a time, or if you meet the class again, they could then focus on the design of the robot's shell. Would they want it to look vaguely human?

A variation on this could be to use the television programmes *Robot Wars* and *Techno Games* for ideas for robot building. In *Robot Wars* the robots were designed to be gladiators, competing against each other in order to destroy or disable the opponent. Each team built robots with different features: an axe-wielding arm or a chainsaw. Some dominated by size, whilst others were small and easily manoeuvrable. *Techno Games* featured robots built to excel at a particular sport, from swimming to gymnastics. More information on these can be found at www.bbc.co.uk/sn/tvradio/programmes/robots/index. shtml and www.five.tv/home/frameset/?content=4465691.

Further information on robots can be found at www.robot.org.uk

Physical education

If you are asked to cover a PE lesson, this often means sitting in a classroom with a class of children who were ready to run around for an hour. Some of them may be glad that they haven't got to try and wangle their way out of the lesson with a 'lost my kit' excuse, but others may have been looking forward to getting wet and muddy. Another consideration is that you may well have a single-sex group of pupils. Late-comers could well claim to have been wandering back from the changing rooms because they didn't know where to go. Here are some ideas to keep them occupied for an hour or so.

o Invent and market a new sport. Pupils should combine two existing sports to make a new one. Once you start to think about it, lots of sports seem to be combinations of others: is polo just hockey on horseback? The new sport needs a name, a set of rules, a drawing or description of the pitch or place that it'll be played on or in, a sketch of the kit worn when playing it, and writing or pictures showing the equipment needed to play it. This could become project work over several lessons or a double lesson. You could ask pupils to come up with one more piece of information at a time to keep up the pace of the lesson, or you could let them work at their own pace and give them a selection of tasks to choose from to include in their project.

o Design a new sports kit. Make this a competitive activity by having a judging and assessment session towards the end of the lesson. Pupils should design a new school PE kit for winter or summer, or both. Or they could design a kit especially for their favourite sport. Set a time limit on the drawing and labelling, and then spread the pictures around on the desks. Ask pupils to make scorecards with categories such as 'practicality' and 'eye-catching'. Collate the scores and then have a ballot or vote to decide on the most popular design.

o Design a one-day Olympics. Pupils are told that they have one stadium and one other venue available (e.g. a river for rowing, rapids for canoeing, an ice rink, etc.). Their stadium can host up to ten events in one day: what will they schedule? They can argue their cases in groups or on paper. Other tasks they can complete as part of this idea include: designing a flag for their Olympics that incorporates the current Olympic logo; planning the needs of spectators, athletes and staff. If this seems too far-reaching, they could plan a sports day for their old junior school instead.

SPORTS NUTRITION

This idea is especially suited to GCSE groups and above, and you may get further ideas by looking at the section on food technology. If you have access to computers, let the pupils try their hands at sports nutrition on this website: www.sycd.co.uk/good-to-eat/#, for which the computers need to have Flash installed. The site concentrates on the nutritional needs of a Manchester United football player. The idea is to choose the healthy food options from drop-down menus and then check them against the 'nutrigauge' which shows how healthy or otherwise they are.

Pupils can check the nutritional content of what they eat every day at this website: nat.crgq.com. They can work out the healthier options and plan a daily or weekly diet for participants in different types of sport. They will need to consider what the competitor will require from their diet, such as energy-giving food, and how this will change if the player plays in more or fewer games, etc. They can write up their findings in a report, or produce an illustrated menu for their chosen sportsperson.

A simpler way to use this website is for pupils to input their own details into the energy calculator, which then tells them how many calories they need in an average day. They could then plan their own healthy diet for a day or week. You can add variables to keep pace in the lesson: tell them that they will be playing an extra hour of football one day and must adapt their menu to include enough energy to sustain them through the game.

You can still have a lesson on sports nutrition without computers: give the group a list of foods off the top of your head and ask them to colour code them red, amber or green depending on whether they shouldn't be eaten regularly, should be eaten in moderation, or can be eaten all the time. After a general consensus, the pupils can use their colour-coded lists to create menus or diet sheets.